Beyond Sectarianism

Christian Mission and Modern Culture

EDITED BY
ALAN NEELY, H. WAYNE PIPKIN,
AND WILBERT R. SHENK

In the series:

Beyond Sectarianism

Re-Imagining Church and World

PHILIP D. KENNESON

TRINITY PRESS INTERNATIONAL
Harrisburg, Pennsylvania

Trinity Press International, P.O. Box 1321, Harrisburg, PA 17105

Trinity Press International is a division of the Morehouse Group.

Copyright © 1999 by Philip D. Kenneson

Biblical quotations are from the New Revised Standard Version of the Bible, copyright 1989 by the Division of Christian Education of the National Council of the Churches of Christ in the USA. Used by permission. All rights reserved.

Cover design: Brian Preuss

Library of Congress Cataloging-in-Publication Data

Kenneson, Philip D.
   Beyond sectarianism ; re-imagining church and world / Philip D. Kenneson.
      p.   cm.
   Includes bibliographical references.
   ISBN 1-56338-278-4 (pbk. : alk. paper)
   1. Church and the world.   I. Title.   II. Series.
BR115.W6K44   1999
261'.1 – dc21   99-27848

Printed in the United States of America

99   00   01   02   03   04   10   9   8   7   6   5   4   3   2   1

For those Christians over the years
who have sought to live faithful lives
and, in so doing,
have been scorned for being "sectarian"

Contents

Preface to the Series

Both Christian mission and modern culture, widely regarded as antagonists, are in crisis. The emergence of the
modern mission movement in the early nineteenth century
cannot be understood apart from the rise of technocratic
society. Now, at the end of the twentieth century, both
modern culture and Christian mission face an uncertain
future.

One of the developments integral to modernity was the
way the role of religion in culture was redefined. Whereas
religion had played an authoritative role in the culture of
Christendom, modern culture was highly critical of religion and increasingly secular in its assumptions. A sustained
effort was made to banish religion to the backwaters of
modern culture.

The decade of the 1980s witnessed further momentous
developments on the geopolitical front with the collapse of
communism. In the aftermath of the breakup of the system of power blocs that dominated international relations
for a generation, it is clear that religion has survived even
if its institutionalization has undergone deep change and
its future forms are unclear. Secularism continues to oppose
religion, while technology has emerged as a major source
of power and authority in modern culture. Both confront
Christian faith with fundamental questions.

The purpose of this series is to probe these developments

from a variety of angles with a view to helping the church
understand its missional responsibility to a culture in crisis. One important resource is the church's experience of
two centuries of cross-cultural mission that has reshaped
the church into a global Christian *ecumene.* The focus of
our inquiry will be the church in modern culture. The series
(1) examines modern/postmodern culture from a missional
point of view; (2) develops the theological agenda that the
church in modern culture must address in order to recover
its own integrity; and (3) tests fresh conceptualizations of
the nature and mission of the church as it engages modern
culture. In other words, these volumes are intended to be
a forum where conventional assumptions can be challenged
and alternative formulations explored.

This series is a project authorized by the Institute of
Mennonite Studies, research agency of the Associated
Mennonite Biblical Seminary, and supported by a generous
grant from the Pew Charitable Trusts.

Editorial Committee

ALAN NEELY
H. WAYNE PIPKIN
WILBERT R. SHENK

Introduction

The Charge of Sectarianism

> But this I admit to you, that according to the Way, which they call a sect (*hairesis*), I worship the God of our ancestors, believing everything laid down according to the law or written in the prophets.
>
> — Acts 24:14

As the twentieth century closes, Christian churches struggle to embody a faithful witness to Jesus Christ within Western societies. What does it mean to be the church in the postmodern West? Though no clear consensus has yet emerged, most Christians do acknowledge one important feature of contemporary Western societies: the church, despite its pretensions in some places, is no longer in reality closely aligned with those power structures that shape the everyday lives of most citizens. One need only reflect on the previous fifteen hundred years of Christendom in the West, years during which the church exercised far-reaching power, to recognize the importance of this change. As many Christians in the West well realize, Christendom is dead, even if its residual impact on the Christian imagination is not. Yet old habits die hard, and many Christians continue to assume that the church cannot be effective unless it regains the reins of power. Other Christians, however, view the end of Christendom not as an event to bemoan but as a welcome opportunity. For these Christians, the collapse of Christendom is painfully but necessarily forcing the church to reassess what it means to be Christ's body in this time and place.

Although it is too soon to evaluate the results of that reassessment, two issues do seem clear. First, the church in this post-Christendom era will need different models for conceptualizing its own identity and its relationship to the rest of society. Second, there is little agreement about which ones might be most promising or about how best to evaluate competing ones. Several different models have already been proposed, and there are certainly more on the horizon. But how will the church discern which of these best encourage faithful embodiments of the gospel in Western societies?

One of the proposed models insists that the church's role in contemporary society is to serve as a "contrast-society" (Lohfink 1984). According to this model, the church is called to be animated by a different spirit than that which animates "the world." By allowing its life to be ordered by a different story, a different set of convictions, and a different set of practices, the church is enabled to embody before the world a distinct social/political alternative. For advocates of such an understanding of the church, this model has tremendous missional promise: it reminds the church that its witness to the world is not something separate from its own embodied existence in the midst of that world. In short, the church must attend to the character of its embodied life because that embodied life *is* its witness to the world.

This promising model has articulate and thoughtful advocates in nearly every confessional branch of Christianity.

Yet many people have serious concerns about such a model of the church. The notion of the church as a contrast-society is rejected by many Christians and non-Christians because it is believed to be too "sectarian." Such charges have often led to little more than heated debates about whether a certain model was or was not sectarian. Rather than evaluating the degree to which particular proposals should be so labeled, this volume offers a different tack.

I begin by asking a more fundamental question: What are we claiming about a particular group when we charge it with being sectarian? As the opening chapter attempts to demonstrate, the answer to that question hinges on the context within which the charge is made. The language of "sects" and "sectarianism" has many different homes. As a result, what a sociologist of religion may mean by labeling a group a "sect" may differ markedly from what a newspaper, a court of law, a contemporary philosopher, or a theologian might mean. Different sets of assumptions and purposes inform these varied charges of sectarianism, and I propose that identifying and distinguishing them might bring a measure of clarity to discussions often mired in name-calling.

Critics who regard as sectarian a church that sets itself in contrast to society assume a complex set of premises in order for this allegation to be both intelligible and damning. I argue in chapter 2 that these critics operate with what many regard as untenable understandings of rationality, culture, politics, religion, and critique. If the intellectual underpinnings of the charge of sectarianism are indeed crumbling, then we are freed to examine both what it might mean for the churches in the West to live as contrast-societies and what difference this might make for their witness to the world. I offer in the final chapter a few preliminary reflections on how moving "beyond sectarianism" allows us to see afresh and unhindered some of the missional promise of the church-as-contrast-society model.

It is my hope that this brief examination of sectarianism will aid churches in discerning faithful ways of being Christ's church in the future that God is bringing. That future will undoubtedly require that Christians continue to debate rigorously what Christ's church should look like and how it should understand itself and its mission. I hope that this volume will help facilitate those important discussions by making it more difficult for them to be short-circuited by unwarranted charges of sectarianism.

I consider it a privilege to thank several people for their help. As is the case with most books, writing this one was not a solo effort but a joint project. My teaching and writing continue to be possible only because my spouse, Kim, works hard to create time and space for them, often at considerable sacrifice. I have also received considerable support and encouragement in thinking through this volume from several colleagues and friends. The following were gracious enough to read and comment on an earlier draft: Craig Farmer, Stan Hauerwas, Susan Higgins, Alan Kreider, J. Lee Magness, Frederick Norris, Jon Stock, James Street, Charles Taber, C. Robert Wetzel, and Paul Williams. This volume is stronger as a result of their suggestions. Had I been wise enough to incorporate all of them, it undoubtedly would have been stronger still. Three other friends deserve special mention. I am deeply indebted to David Cunningham, who devoted considerable energy to improving the argument of this book. Of most importance, he single-handedly persuaded me that a line of argument I had earlier abandoned was indeed the way to proceed. Margaret Adam and Andrew Adam read my earliest ruminations on these matters over a period of many months; they also fine-tuned the final draft. I likely would not have finished this book had it not been for their enthusiasm and generous support at both ends of this project. Finally, I would like to thank Wilbert Shenk, both for inviting me to write this book and for waiting patiently while I completed it.

1

Different Contexts of Sectarianism

Before the contemporary church and its critics can move "beyond sectarianism," there must be some common understanding about what is presumed when labeling a group a sect. Sorting through this matter is difficult, not least because the language of "sect" is itself vigorously contested, as any student of church history, theology, or the sociology of religion well knows. In an attempt to bring some clarity to this matter, this chapter identifies six different contexts within which the language of "sect," "sectarian," and "sectarianism" is routinely used. Because each of these contexts is itself framed by a different set of narratives, practices, and convictions, these six contexts are not necessarily compatible conceptually. This potential conceptual incompatibility does not, however, keep several of these different usages from being collapsed together; indeed, a particular charge of sectarianism often gains much of its rhetorical power by drawing simultaneously on the pejorative resonances operative in several different contexts. More often than not, this blurring of distinctions clouds the issues under discussion. Hence, this chapter attempts to delineate as clearly as possible these six different contexts within which the language is used, with the hope that the language will either be used in the future with a good deal more precision or be dropped altogether.

Sociological Contexts

In sociological contexts, the language of "sect" is frequently used to denominate a group of people whose beliefs and practices are substantially distinct from those of the host society. In this broad and least pejorative use, the language of sect is employed simply to point to a group whose identifiable patterns of thinking/acting mark them as a distinct minority group. Although there are no universal ways in which groups distinguish themselves *as* groups, the construction and maintenance of their identity usually involves the complex interaction of particular narratives, practices, and convictions.[1] In each case, this peculiar web of narratives, practices, and convictions shapes the lives of this group in ways discernibly different from the webs that inform and form the lives of those outside the sect. Of course, this "inside" of the sect can be contrasted to several different "outsides." For example, many Mennonites would be regarded as a sect with respect to the wider, dominant culture for their refusal to participate in war. Moreover, they might also be regarded as a sect with respect to much of Protestantism. In each case, the Mennonites are viewed as embodying a peculiar web of narratives, practices, and convictions that set them apart to a noticeable degree from other identifiable groups. In short, the use of "sect" language within sociological contexts involves identifying those boundary markers that are necessary for establishing and maintaining minority group identity. This use of "sect" is well summarized by David Kelsey:

Sociologically, a sect is a relatively small group of persons whose beliefs and behavior are sharply differentiated from the surrounding society. . . . Because it is a deviant minority in a larger society, a sect receives no support for its beliefs from the society at large and has to rely on the group's own inner life to provide that support (1990:12).

Although the discipline of sociology (and particularly the sociology of religion) is one context in which sociological uses of the language of sectarianism abound, it is not the only one. Indeed, anyone with an interest in examining what enables a group to distinguish itself as an identifiable minority group can be said to be exploring what are in sociological circles "sectarian" issues. For example, in 1971 the Lutheran theologian and church historian George Lindbeck wrote about what he called "the sectarian future of the church":

The "sectarianism" about which we shall be talking is rather like the "diaspora" which Karl Rahner in particular has so eloquently described. It is a sociological, not an ecclesiological, concept. The mainstream of early Christianity was sectarian in the sense in which we use the term. It consisted of a small, strongly deviant minority, unsupported by cultural convention and prestige, within the larger society (:227; cf. Scroggs 1975).

Lindbeck's comments suggest that the language of sectarianism can be used to designate a minority position without necessarily entailing any criticism of that group. Although this nonpejorative use of the language is often intended in sociological contexts, the fact that writers must usually work very hard to distinguish their usage from more popular and pejorative ones reminds us that the resonances that particular concepts pick up in one context are often transferred to another. A pertinent example of this is the way in which "church" and "sect" are often used as contrasting terms in the relatively young discipline known as the sociology of religion. This habit has been greatly shaped by Max Weber's well-known distinction between church and sect, a distinction on which Ernst Troeltsch later elaborated.[2] Troeltsch's seminal work, *The Social Teaching of the Christian Churches,* offers a three-part typology (church, sect, mysticism) as a way of accounting for the distinct social and ethical expressions of different understandings of Christianity. Troeltsch spends most of his time showing how the history of Christianity and its doctrines can be illuminated by examining the differences between the church-type and the sect-type.

The church-type emphasizes the redemptive features of the Christian tradition, viewing the institution itself as a dispenser of saving grace. This grace is imparted by means of the sacraments administered by the clergy. The church accepts as much of the world as possible as a relative good, using whatever political and economic power it can for its own ends, though to do so it must inevitably compromise the more radical teachings of Jesus. As Troeltsch writes: "The Church-type represents the longing for a universal all-embracing ideal, the desire to control great masses of men, and therefore the urge to dominate the world and civilization in general"; as a result, "the Church found it impossible to avoid making a compromise with the State, with the social order, and with economic conditions" (1960:1:334, 335). Finally, because the church-type locates holiness within the institution, the church does not require its members to follow the divine law in their own lives.[3]

In contrast, says Troeltsch, the sect-type interprets the teachings of Jesus in a straightforward and radical manner, constituting itself as a small, voluntary fellowship of people who seek to embody the divine law in their own lives. The sect stands apart from and in opposition to the world, emphasizing the eschatological elements of Christian doctrine and prohibiting participation in political affairs because it eschews exercising dominion over others. Moreover, a measure of religious equality characterizes the sect, which usually avoids drawing sharp distinctions between clergy and laity. Finally, Troeltsch notes that the sect draws its members primarily from the lower classes.

Troeltsch believed that both the church-type and the sect-type were the "logical result of the Gospel." In fact, he acknowledged that he had very little invested in this specific terminology: for those who objected to it, he was happy to substitute the distinction between "institutional churches and voluntary churches" (:340). Said another way, Troeltsch realized that some Christians believed that being the church required the willingness to stand in protest of and contrast to the wider society, whereas other Christians believed that such a posture was unnecessary if not dangerous. Troeltsch's church-sect typology, therefore, is an attempt to account for these two different attitudes toward the "wider society" that subsequently generated two distinct social ethics.[4]

Subsequent scholars have been extremely critical of Troeltsch's typology. Most criticize Troeltsch's list of defining sectarian traits, offering their own (usually no less idiosyncratic) lists in its place. Indeed, such lists have become so routine and the debate so protracted that it is only a slight exaggeration to claim that there are as many differ-

ent lists of defining sectarian traits as there are sociologists
of religion.[5] Many have also criticized Troeltsch for com-
bining sociological and theological agendas, while others
have pointed out that the typology — far from being de-
scriptively neutral — seems to have descriptive power only
within seventeenth- and eighteenth-century Europe.[6] Still
others, like H. Richard Niebuhr (1929), have pointed to the
static nature of the typology, suggesting instead a more dynamic model that accounts for the ways in which churches
and sects, especially in the United States, are routinely
transformed into denominations (:16–21).[7] Some scholars
have gone even further and argued that denominations are
the organizational form of Troeltsch's less-often-discussed
third type — the highly inward and subjectivistic piety he
calls mysticism.

> While sensing that individual mysticism was the re-
> ligion of the future, Troeltsch could not anticipate
> its organizational form.... In America, however, in-
> dividual mysticism found a fertile soil. Evangelical
> pietism, "the religion of the heart," was the vehicle
> which served to spread individual mysticism, democ-
> ratizing and popularizing it, as it were, throughout
> American Protestantism whereas denominationalism,
> the great American religious invention, became its
> organizational form (Casanova 1994:53).

If a scholarly consensus has emerged within academic
sociology that Troeltsch's church-sect typology is seriously
flawed, this has not kept the typology from wielding enormous influence in other circles. Indeed, the church-sect
typology continues to impact many people's thinking about
the relationship of the church to the surrounding culture.
It is only with this background in mind that we can make

sense of the book which has perhaps shaped the contemporary debate about sectarianism within theological circles more than any other English-language text: H. Richard Niebuhr's *Christ and Culture* (1951). Here, within Niebuhr's influential five-part typology, the so-called sectarians are identified as those who embody a "Christ against Culture" posture:

> Its intention was directed to the achievement of a Christian life, apart from civilization, in obedience to the laws of Christ, and in pursuit of a perfection wholly distinct from the aims that men seek in politics and economics, in science and arts. Protestant sectarianism — to use that term in its narrow, sociological meaning — has given the same sort of answer to the question of Christ and culture. Out of the many sects that arose in the sixteenth and seventeenth centuries, protesting against the worldly church, both Catholic and Protestant, and seeking to live under the Lordship of Christ alone, only a few survive. The Mennonites have come to represent the attitude most purely, since they not only renounce all participation in politics and refuse to be drawn into military service, but follow their own distinctive customs and regulations in economics and education.... Hundreds of other groups, many of them evanescent, and thousands of individuals, have felt themselves compelled by loyalty to Christ to withdraw from culture and to give up all responsibility for the world (:56–57).[8]

This dual charge — of withdrawing from culture and of abnegating responsibility for the world — reverberates through all contemporary critiques of sectarianism. This charge is aimed particularly at those who believe that the gospel calls the church to retain a visible distinction *from* and viable witness *to* the world. We will revisit this dual charge, along with the presuppositions underwriting it, in the next chapter.

In sociological contexts, the language of sectarianism is used to focus attention on the processes and justifications used by minority groups as they seek to retain a distinct identity. In that sense, any minority group that desires to retain a discernible identity is interested in "sectarian" issues, because it must constantly reflect on the cultural dynamics that shape and frame its life. For Christians living in post-Christendom and post-Christian contexts, understanding these dynamics will likely become increasingly important.

Ecclesiological Contexts

Long before sociologists used the language of sectarianism, it was widely employed in ecclesiological contexts. Just as sociologists study sects for reasons that are internal to their discipline, so the church has had its own theological reasons over the years to describe certain groups as sects. The ecclesial context for these concerns involves the character of the church, particularly the historic confession of its unity and catholicity. From its earliest days, the church of Jesus Christ came to confess itself as a unity, as the one Body of Christ (Eph. 4:1–6). As such, threats to that unity were taken as attacks against the integrity of that Body. This partly explains why a clear distinction was not made early on between schismatics and heretics, for both fractured the unity of the church.[9] In many respects, early schismatics like the Novatianists or the Donatists were the first ecclesiological sectarians, even though this terminology was not used at the time.[10] Each side in these early disputes agreed that the critical question concerned the identity and locus of the true church. Where was the true church, and who was inside and outside it? For example, Augustine criticized the Donatists because they, like many schismatics after them, divided the church and then insisted that they themselves were the only true Christians.[11] One of the guiding questions, therefore, in ecclesiological contexts, is: Where is the true church to be found? More often than not, the answer given by schismatics is quite straightforward — with us alone. Or as David Kelsey has suggested, the motto of such sectarians is "No salvation outside (our!) church" (1990:32).

Over the years, ecclesiological uses of the language of sectarianism have been a constant fixture of the American conversation. Part of this stems from the overriding Protestant ethos of the United States, for, as many commentators have noted, fragmentation and schism seem endemic to the Protestant principle. Yet this dangerous feature of Protestantism became all the more so when combined with the individualism, religious freedom, and the exaltation of private judgment that are the hallmark of American life. This was well noted by nineteenth-century European transplants to the United States such as Philip Schaff and his good friend and colleague at Mercersburg Seminary, John W. Nevin (Graham 1995:4–20). The latter wrote a scathing critique of "the sect system" in the United States, insisting that the greatest threat to the Christian faith was the divisiveness of these sects (Nevin 1848).

Nevin and Schaff were certainly right to criticize the schismatic tendencies that marked the church in their day. Yet many Christians today find themselves in a quite different context. With the end of Christendom and the subsequent rise of ecumenism, there has been an increasing attempt on the part of many Christians to emphasize their similarities with other Christians rather than their differences. Nevertheless, even in an ecumenical age there continue to be churches that operate with this form of sectarian spirit and so view ecumenical cooperation as a form of compromise. This kind of sectarianism appears to be what sociologist Bryan Wilson is pointing to when he makes the following comment: "Although ecumenical tendencies dominate the contemporary religious scene in Britain, and are increasingly important in America, there persist a variety of movements within Christianity which manifest no immediate ecumenical disposition. These are the sects" (1966:179).

In sum, the language of sectarianism has often been used in ecclesial contexts to identify those disposed toward schism and fragmentation. Those so disposed have been resoundingly and rightly criticized from the beginning for their threat to the church's unified witness to the world. Although the debate between Augustine and the Donatists reminds us that it is often difficult to discern which party is fostering schism, both sides were right in their determination that the true church not be divided.

Theological Contexts

Some Christian groups distinguish themselves from other Christians on the basis of doctrine or polity, yet continue to acknowledge the legitimacy of other embodiments and expressions of the Christian faith. In the United States, such groups are routinely labeled "denominations." That such groups are rarely regarded as sects suggests the peace that most American Christians have made with a fragmented church. Yet not everyone has viewed the proliferation of denominations as a benign development. Nevin's diatribe against "the sect system" was not limited to those groups who were schismatic and who believed they alone possessed the truth. Nevin also lashed out against any group that "professes to look upon itself only as a tribe of the true Israel, a section or wing in the sacramental host of God's elect," and yet goes on "to arrogate to itself within its own bounds full church powers; such powers as have no meaning except as conditioned by the idea of a catholic or whole church" (1848:163). In short, Nevin saw that denominations made a mockery of the catholicity of the church.

From whence come these theological divisions? Contemporary histories, often informed by the sociology of religion, have tended to emphasize the social, political, and psychological factors contributing to their rise, almost to the exclusion of theological rationale. Although it is certainly true that the reasons for division were more complicated (and perhaps less lofty) than the reasons often given by the "separatists," such an admission hardly justifies the current trend of discounting all theological rationale in favor of "more fundamental" factors.

The Scriptures of the New Testament suggest that the early churches shared no singular theological system; indeed, the New Testament evinces little concern for system at all, manifesting instead considerable diversity of theological perspective. But this diversity is not without limits, as the process of canon formation alone reminds us. Though the early churches seem to have left room for both theological diversity and disagreement, it was not long before some groups (such as the Montanists) came to understand themselves as distinct, based upon a rationale that was at least partly theological. These groups usually understood themselves as serving a prophetic or reforming role within the rest of the church, thereby attempting to justify theologically their status as a distinct group. This suggests why theological use of the language of sectarianism is often so closely tied to sociological and ecclesiological uses, for part of the obligation of any minority group is to specify clearly the larger group or groups (including churches) from which it desires to distinguish itself. For example, the New Testament itself may be read as legitimating this way of thinking in that it served some early followers of Jesus in distinguishing themselves from other Jewish communities and traditions.

Something like this theological context seems to be assumed when the word *hairesis* (often translated as "sect") is used in the New Testament. There the sects identified include the sect of the Pharisees (Acts 15:5; 26:5), the sect of the Sadducees (Acts 5:17), and the sect of the Nazarenes (Acts 24:5). This last sect, it will be remembered, is the one of which Paul was accused of being the ringleader when he was brought before Felix the governor. In each of these cases we have distinguishable groups whose disagreements with each other partly define what it means to be Jewish in the first century. As Alasdair MacIntyre helpfully reminds us, vital traditions always embody "continuities of conflict" (1984:222). Thus, centrally important to Jewish identity is an ongoing argument about what being Jewish has entailed in the past, what it currently entails, and what it ought to entail in the future. The same, of course, might be said with respect to Christian identity.

It should be noted that these first three uses of the language of sectarianism point to phenomena that have a long history within Christianity. Moreover, the contexts cannot be neatly separated, because the church's life and witness before the world cannot be neatly divided into sociological, ecclesiological, and theological components. Nevertheless, these different contexts often emphasize different aspects of the church's life. As a means of clarifying each, we might note some of the different historical relationships among them. On the contemporary scene, these three senses sometimes coincide, even though it is arguable that they do so less often now than in the past. Some would argue, for example, that the Boston Church of Christ is sectarian in all three senses.[12] It would be a mistake, however, to assume either that these three senses of sectarianism have always coincided historically, or that they need do so logically (or theologically). For example, many Franciscans and Mennonites could be regarded as sectarians in the sociological and theological senses even though most have not been sectarians in the ecclesiological sense. Many "mainline" or "oldline" denominations in the United States (such as the United Methodists and Presbyterians) have been sectarians in the theological sense without being so in either the sociological or ecclesiological ones. On these historical variations Lindbeck has made perhaps the most helpful observations:

> In later centuries . . . when the majority of people became Christian, sociological and theological sectarianism necessarily coincided, rather than doing so only occasionally as in the first centuries (e.g., in the case of the Montanists). Once a deviant minority within the larger society became one which also fragmented the *corpus Christianum*, it naturally tended to insist on a particular and narrow interpretation of Christianity and to recruit its adherents from a single racial, social or cultural group. In other words, it almost inevitably added to its sociological sectarianism the theological and ecclesiological aspects as well. Conversely, when what a Roman Catholic might regard

as theological sects were not sociological ones, as was true of the larger Protestant bodies, they tended toward some degree of comprehensiveness or catholicity (1971:227–28).

In short, although the first three senses are often inextricably woven together to construct the fabric of a particular group's identity, they need not be so. As Lindbeck suggests, Roman Catholics might regard many Protestant denominations as sectarian in the theological sense, even if they are not necessarily sectarian in the sociological or ecclesiological ones. This suggests that contemporary churches in the West could without contradiction seek to be sociologically distinguishable from the wider culture, doctrinally distinguishable from other Christian communities, yet also ecumenical and catholic.

Epistemological Contexts

A quite different context for the charge of sectarianism has emerged in the cauldron of late modernity. As its name suggests, the context involves claims about the character of knowledge. Those charged with being epistemological sectarians argue that knowledge claims and their justifications are always rooted in particular, tradition-dependent assumptions, rather than in universal, tradition-independent ones. Most so-called epistemological sectarians presuppose and endorse the contemporary critique of foundationalism.

Foundationalism is the view that propositions are of two kinds, those which stand in need of evidence, and those which provide the required evidence. The latter are said to be foundational, since they do not stand in need of further evidence.... Foundationalism is the view that a belief is a rational belief only if it is related, in appropriate ways, to a set of propositions which constitute the foundations of what we believe (Phillips 1995:xiii, 3).

In contrast, nonfoundationalism argues that the search for tradition-free grounding of human knowledge and practice is chimerical, because any criteria for dividing up foundational propositions from those requiring further justification will themselves be products of a certain tradition of inquiry.[13] From a nonfoundationalist perspective, therefore, knowledge is considered inseparable from particular communities whose narratives, practices, and convictions make the production as well as the retrieval of knowledge possible and intelligible. Hence, as Ronald Thiemann rightly argues, justifying Christian faith is an activity that takes place *within* Christian communities rather than from some putatively neutral or disinterested position: "'The Christian faith' is that set of beliefs and practices which in their social and historical reality provide the context for arguments about which beliefs and practices ought so to function" (1985:73). If all knowledge and justification is tradition dependent in this way, then there is always the possibility (though not the inevitability) that any attempt either to untether such knowledge claims from their traditions or to translate them into some other tradition will result in a loss of coherence or intelligibility of those claims. For example, one might argue that much of the specific character of Christian forgiveness and reconciliation is lost once these concrete practices are stripped of their Christian particularities and inserted within a different set of narratives, practices, and convictions, such as those associated with therapeutic psychology (Jones 1995).

This rejection of universal epistemologies cuts across disciplinary boundaries. In theological circles this position is commonly associated with so-called postliberal theologians.[14] Because much of the next two chapters draws on postliberal insights, a brief account of postliberalism is in order. George Lindbeck, one of the most prominent advocates of postliberal theology, argues that the Christian faith is best understood as a cultural-linguistic system. As such, the Christian faith provides an idiom for "construing reality, expressing experience, and ordering life" (1984:47–48). By viewing the Christian faith as an idiom, "a comprehensive scheme or story used to structure all dimensions of existence," postliberalism insists that Christianity is not *primarily* either a set of propositions to be believed or a set of inner experiences to be expressed. Rather, the Christian faith is viewed as "the medium in which one moves, a set of skills that one employs in living one's life" (:35). One of the most important implications of this model is that it suggests that becoming a Christian is more akin to learning a language than to assenting to a set of propositions or to having some kind of religious experience.

Postliberalism also insists that the canonical texts of Scripture are at the heart of this cultural-linguistic system. As Lindbeck writes: "For those who are steeped in them [canonical writings], no world is more real than the ones they create. A scriptural world is thus able to absorb the universe. It supplies the interpretive framework within which believers seek to live their lives and understand reality" (:117; cf. Frei 1974). Hence, postliberalism does not encourage believers to "find their stories in the Bible, but rather that they make the story of the Bible *their* story.... Intratextual theology redescribes reality within the scriptural framework rather than translating

Scripture into extrascriptural categories. It is the text, so to speak, which absorbs the world, rather than the world the text" (:118).

If postliberals view the Christian faith as a cultural-linguistic system, they regard Christian doctrine primarily as the "grammar" that regulates communities of practice. As such, doctrine shapes and is shaped by, among other things, the church's more primary language — such as its language in worship. So, for example, the doctrine of the Trinity is first of all a guide to the worshiping community about how to address the God it worships. But it did not fall from the sky; it developed through a lengthy engagement with those worship practices of the community. By suggesting that doctrine serves a primarily regulative function as the grammar of the Christian community, postliberals remind us that doctrine plays a crucial but subordinate role in communities of faith. Just as grammar books do not themselves create communities of language users, so church doctrine does not by itself create communities of faith. Anyone who has tried to learn a foreign language knows that the best way to learn one is to immerse one's self into a community of competent language users. When that is not possible, we do what we believe is the next best thing: we attempt to acquire the language by learning its constitutive parts, including its formal grammar. The parallel is important. The best way to "learn" the Christian faith is to immerse one's self into a community of competent practitioners who are themselves involved in internalizing the grammar of the faith, even if they can articulate little formal doctrine. If that is not possible, then one might do what is arguably the next best thing: study Christian doctrine — the grammar of the Christian faith — to get an idea of how Christian discourse and practice hang together.

Postliberal theologians insist that knowledge is best understood as local knowledge, and that the acquisition of knowledge cannot be separated from initiation into and formation by a community whose convictions, practices, and narratives grant that knowledge its intelligibility. Critics of postliberal theology insist that such an understanding of epistemology leads to a view of the Christian faith that is dangerous. Many of these critics, who charge postliberals with being sectarian in this epistemological sense, believe that such a position inevitably leads to fideism, relativism, tribalism, obscurantism, and religious totalitarianism. These criticisms will be addressed in the next chapter.

Legal Contexts

The charge of sectarianism acquires many of its negative resonances through its use and function within two powerful institutional frameworks: the judiciary system and public education. Although these two institutional systems differ in substantial ways with regard to their function and purpose within American society, they appear to share several assumptions about "sectarian" issues. Indeed, many of the discussions of such issues in the courts have concerned the role of "religious" issues in public education. As a result, these two powerful institutions have greatly shaped not only specific discussions of sectarianism, but also certain images and assumptions about it that have subsequently reverberated throughout the wider culture.

During the last third of the nineteenth century, the United States accelerated its experiment in public education. This experiment was fueled partly by widespread concern over the influx of Irish (Roman Catholic) immigrants during the middle of the century and the desire to assimilate them into American (largely Protestant) culture.[15] Even at an early stage in the development of public schools, there was widespread consensus that they should not be directly or indirectly involved in the teaching of religion;[16] however, this consensus also included the belief that a "nonsectarian" pan-Protestantism, which was embodied by daily Bible reading and prayer in the schools, was not only permissible but desirable. Thus in 1859 a Boston judge dismissed charges against a public school teacher who had whipped a young Roman Catholic boy until he agreed to read the Ten Commandments from the King James Version of the Bible — a version that Roman Catholics at the time were forbidden by canon law to read because of its anti-Catholic slant, as evidenced by its reference to the pope as the "man of sin" in the dedicatory preface. In his decision in *Commonwealth* v. *Cooke*, the judge argued:

> The Bible has long been in our common schools. It was placed there by our fathers, not for the purpose of teaching sectarian religion, but a knowledge of God and His will, whose practice is religion. It was placed there as the book best adapted from which to "teach children and youth the principles of piety, justice and a sacred regard for truth, love to their country, humanity, and a universal benevolence, sobriety, moderation and temperance, and those other virtues which are the ornaments of human society, and the basis upon which a republic constitution is founded." But in doing this, no scholar is requested to believe it, none to receive it as the only true version of the laws of God. The teacher enters into no argument to prove its correctness, and gives no instructions in theology from it. To read the Bible in school for these and like

purposes, or to require it to be read without sectarian explanations, is no interference with religious liberty (Pfeffer 1975:177).

In these and other early cases involving church-state issues, the language of sectarianism is used almost synonymously with Protestant denominationalism; as such, there seems to be considerable overlap between this usage and that used in theological contexts. For example, the Supreme Court of Illinois in *Williams* v. *Stanton School District* (1917) wrote: "The constitution not only forbids the appropriation for any purpose or in any manner of the common school funds to sectarian or denominational institutions, but it contemplates that the separation between the common school and the sectarian or denominational school or institution shall be so open, notorious and complete that there can be no room for reasonable doubt that the common school is absolutely free from the influence, control or domination of the sectarian institution" (Stokes 1950:2:71). Thus at this early stage the courts were concerned that no identifiably religious group would be able to advance its particular and distinctive teachings through use of public funds (either state or federal). However, this habit of equating "sectarian" with "that which is peculiar to a specific denomination" and "nonsectarian" with pan-Protestantism — with what all Protestants supposedly had in common — was only possible as long as Protestantism continued to be granted normative status throughout the United States. In fact, some have argued that the flight from public schools by Roman Catholics and Jews at the end of the Second World War was an attempt to avoid the Protestant ethos that continued to dominate public education.[17] This widespread habit of considering "Protestantism and Americanism as inseparable and interchangeable" became more problematic with increased immigration and a growing sensitivity to ethnic and minority groups.[18]

Once this emerging pluralism began to be formally recognized and legally established, official state-sponsored school prayers were held to be unconstitutional. One such landmark case was *Engel* v. *Vitale* (1962). At issue was whether the New York Board of Regents, in an attempt to further "Moral and Spiritual Values," could compose and recommend for widespread adoption the following "nonsectarian" public school prayer: "Almighty God, we acknowledge our dependence upon Thee, and we beg Thy blessing upon us, our parents, our teachers and our Country" (Mathisen 1982:352). The court ruled that the noncompulsory and nondenominational character of the recommended prayer was beside the point, and that such prayers violated the Establishment Clause of the First Amendment.

This case, along with several other church-state cases in the early 1960s, highlighted what many people knew prior to this decision but were hesitant to admit — that the dream of an American society held together by some form of religious unity was no longer tenable. Such lowest-common-denominator religion was offensive not only to atheists and nonbelievers, but also to adherents of particular traditions. For example, Arthur Gilbert argued powerfully at the time that the genericness of America's "nonsectarian" religion undercut the particularity of the Jewish faith. He wrote:

> Jews believe, for example, that when a faith in God is taught, it must be achieved in the context of historical associations accompanied by religious rites and

symbols that are related to that particular religious group. Indeed, God *is* Father of all men. Yet we want our children to know God as the God of Abraham, Isaac and Jacob, as the God who freed the Hebrews from slavery. We do not appreciate the vague and un-defined God to which the "American religion" offers lip service. We do not want our children to think of God only in abstract terms, nor in Christian terms. We want the education concerning God to take place within the context of Jewish association and experi-ence, so that when the image of God is invoked, it is associated in our children's minds with the experiences of the Hebrew people. It is impossible to teach such a God in the public schools. . . . Most of the so-called non-sectarian rites that are now practiced in the public schools are Christian in form. . . . Think for a moment of yourself as a Jewish parent. Your six-year-old child comes home from the public schools and stands up for the Kadish ceremony, sanctifying the Sabbath, and he bows his head and folds his hands. Christians might think this very nice and charming, such a splendid picture of innocent, youthful devotion. But the Jewish parent is offended. This is not how Jews pray, with head lowered and hands folded. This is the Chris-tian form of prayer that the child had learned in the public school. As much as you appreciate the spirit of thanksgiving fostered by the school, you are hard put to it because you have to undo tactfully the whole manner of prayer imposed in the public school ritual (1961:428).

The increasingly widespread recognition that the United States was not merely a Protestant nation, but a nation that was home to people of many different faiths and convictions, made it all but inevitable that the language of sectarianism in its legal sense would become less and less helpful. In short, the legal notion of sectarianism only makes sense if a coherent sense of nonsectarianism remains. But as one commentator has rightly noted, once the ideal of religious unity was abandoned, the whole concept of nonsectarianism became unusable (Tegborg 1978:170).

Hence a subtle but important shift has taken place during the last half-century. Prior to this shift, in the midst of a society that remained residually Protestant, the contrast between "nonsectarian" and "sectarian" religion referred primarily to the degree of genericness of any given expression of Protestant Christianity. With the increasingly pluralistic character of the American cultural landscape, the U.S. Supreme Court came to use the term "sectarian" with less frequency; however, when the term was used, it was often used as a synonym for "religious." Hence, when ruling on educational issues, the Court has referred both to religious schools and colleges and to the fundamental convictions that inform these institutions as "sectarian." For example, in *Grand Rapids School District* v. *Ball* (1985), Justice William J. Brennan, writing for the majority, asserted the following:

> Our inquiry must begin with a consideration of the nature of the institutions in which the [Title I] programs operate. Of the forty-one private schools where these "part-time public schools" have operated, forty are *identifiably religious schools.* . . . Given that forty of the forty-one schools in this case are thus *"pervasively sectarian,"* the challenged public-school programs operating in the religious schools may imper-

missibly advance religion (Eastland 1993:374; emphasis added).

What is striking about this usage is the way it equates the technical legal term "pervasively sectarian" with the phrase "identifiably religious." As noted already, to label something as sectarian requires that there be a normative mainstream from which sectarians deviate. The assumption by the Court seems to be that being part of the mainstream entails being "secular." This reinforces the widespread assumption that being secular is synonymous with being open, rational, and inclusive, whereas almost by definition being religious or sectarian involves being narrow, dogmatic, and parochial. Particularly bothersome is the way in which those religious institutions have themselves accepted such labels, routinely referring to themselves, for example, as sectarian or parochial schools.

These are but two examples of how social institutions may contribute to establishing the "grammar" of sectarianism. By placing their enormous authority behind their usage, social institutions (like the judicial and educational systems) shape the way average citizens think about such matters. Moreover, the negative resonances generated by these institutions with respect to "sectarianism" often make it difficult for anyone so labeled to be taken seriously.

Media Contexts

The media in the West are unrivaled in their ability to shape public opinion. Indeed, their enormous authority and putative neutrality often combine to sustain certain notions that are far from being purely descriptive. That the media are themselves purveyors of certain convictions can be seen in the way the electronic and print media routinely refer to any group that deviates from a relatively circumscribed under-standing of establishment religion as a "sect" or "cult." The cumulative effect of such usage is to raise serious suspicions about anyone who holds deep "religious" convictions, par-ticularly when those convictions encourage behavior that is generally regarded as ancillary or contrary to the "proper" (culturally circumscribed) concerns of "religion." In this way, people who are accused (and this language itself is telling) of being members of sects or cults are regularly considered by the general public as "religious fanatics."[19]

For example, a computer search of Associated Press sto-ries from a six-month period yielded fourteen different stories where "cult" and "sect" were used interchangeably. Several of these stories, which ran during the first six months of 1994, concerned the trial of eleven Branch Da-vidians from Waco, Texas, who were charged with the shooting deaths of four government officers in February 1993. One such story contained the following background paragraph about the fire that destroyed the Branch David-ian "compound," as it was commonly referred to by the media: "The fire ended a standoff that began Feb. 28, 1993, with a gunbattle between the *sect* and the federal Bureau of Alcohol, Tobacco and Firearms. As many as 86 *cult* members are believed to have died in the inferno."[20] Sim-ilarly, the lead paragraph of an Associated Press story a few months later showed the same propensity to use the terms synonymously: "A federal agent who infiltrated the Branch Davidian *sect* before an unsuccessful raid is suing a news-paper and a TV station, claiming they caused the gun battle between agents and the *cultists*."[21]

Lest these two examples from the Waco incident be taken as aberrations, consider the opening two paragraphs of this Associated Press story filed from Jerusalem: "A 25–hour standoff between police and armed *cult* members in suburban Tel Aviv ended today when *sect* members surrendered. Over three dozen people had been holed up in the *cult's* compound since early Tuesday, when hundreds of police moved onto the stronghold to arrest the charismatic *sect* leader and about 50 of his followers in a heated pre-dawn gun battle."[22]

The clear message communicated by the media when the language of sect or sectarian is employed is that these people are at best extremists and at worst dangerous. Thus it should come as no surprise that this six-month survey of Associated Press usage showed that the adjective "sectarian" most commonly modifies the word "violence," though "sectarian" was also used to modify the following: "conflict," "rivalries," "shooting," "dissent," "suspicions," "trouble," "killings," "strife," "passions," "fighting," and "disturbances." By citing these examples of usage, I in no way intend to suggest that they are in every case unwarranted; rather, my aim is to state explicitly what most people already assume: to be identified as a member of a sect (or a cult, for the two are so often synonymous) is to be identified as being well outside the mainstream of what the media (and likely a majority of citizens) consider to be "respectable religion." In its almost uniformly pejorative use of "sect," the media contribute to the negative image the general populace has of anyone who dares challenge widely accepted cultural norms, particularly as these relate to religion's proper bounds.

Delineating these different contexts of sectarianism makes visible a certain shift that has taken place, especially during the last quarter century. With increased secularization in the West and the collapse of Christendom, churches that have desired to retain a distinctively Christian identity have increasingly and almost necessarily had to understand themselves as sectarian in the sociological sense. Indeed, it is arguable that there is a direct correlation between an acceptance of the collapse of Christendom and a willingness to accept this description. But with this shift has come a parallel shift in the way in which sectarianism is identified and criticized. In many contemporary settings, calling a group "sectarian" has little or nothing to do with the perceived threat that they pose to the church's unity and witness. Instead, labeling certain groups "sectarian" serves to ridicule them for refusing to engage the world on the world's terms.

Many people across denominational and confessional lines are beginning to understand that the Western churches in late modernity might need, for the sake of faithful witness, to retrieve the biblical notion of the people of God as a contrast-society (Lohfink 1984). This would require the church to assume a posture that is, in Lindbeck's words, both "catholic and sociologically sectarian" (1971:228). Moreover, the plausibility, if not also the desirability, of such a posture for the church could be reinforced by describing the church as sectarian in the epistemological sense as well. However, any attempt to put forward a constructive and positive sense of sectarianism will have to overcome the pejorative connotations that have accrued to the term over the years and that continue to accrue to it in its various contexts. Given this complicated and confused situation, perhaps Christians and non-Christians alike might eschew the language of sectarianism altogether, choosing instead to find other ways of describing what they find commendable or objectionable. For Christians, this might encourage a thorough rethinking of its self-understanding, particularly as it concerns its relationship to "the world." But before we can take up that constructive project, we must examine the presuppositions that make many of the contemporary charges of sectarianism so damning. Unless the accusatory tone of these charges can be shown to be unwarranted, most churches will remain wary of openly embracing a posture that can easily be labeled "sectarian."

2

The Presuppositions
Behind the Contemporary Charge

Laying bare the unstated assumptions that underwrite a particular charge of sectarianism is slow and demanding work. Yet such work is indispensable. If many of the presuppositions that have funded such charges in the past are now suspect, as I believe they are, this may lead us to inquire to what extent contemporary charges of sectarianism remain coherent. Presently, those most often accused of being sectarian are those who advocate that the church in the West understand itself as a contrast-society. This chapter focuses on the presuppositions of those critics who label such a position "sectarian" and who in so doing believe they have rendered such a position untenable. Although most of the presuppositions examined below are closely interrelated and cannot be neatly separated, for heuristic purposes I have grouped them under five broad headings.

The Real Community as Universal and Rational

As the previous chapter has argued, for much of the church's history being a sectarian was considered an offense against the church. Schism was a direct affront to the church's confessed unity and catholicity. The contemporary context, however, is quite different. Those who routinely criticize the church-as-contrast-society model and its advocates do not do so because they believe that this model threatens the church's unity and catholicity. Rather, critics who label this model "sectarian" assume that a broader, more fundamental, more "inclusive" community has precedence over what they take to be the narrow, contingent, and more "exclusive" community of the church.

These critics consider as sectarian any attempt to establish or maintain a distinct Christian identity through initiation into a different set of practices, convictions, and sustaining narratives. For these critics, forming the church as a contrast-society inevitably entails withdrawing from the wider, ostensibly more fundamental "human community." Here the assumption is that some universal community in the abstract has clear priority over any concrete, particular community of persons. For example, the church-as-contrast-society has been labeled as sectarian for removing the church "from the life and death policy issues of *the human community*" (Miscamble 1987:73; emphasis added). But where is this singular, monolithic human community, and what makes it a community? All identifiable communities share something in common; this is what shapes them as the communities they are. But those who speak about the importance of this "human community," and the threat that particular communities presumably pose to it, rarely articulate what these commonalties are. As a result, many of the same people who routinely criticize "sectarians" for talking about an idealized ecclesial community that remains largely invisible do so in the interest of preserving what is arguably much less visible — something called *the* human community.

In a similar way, Christians who focus on maintaining a distinct identity are routinely castigated for participating less than wholeheartedly in the "wider" cultural conversation of a given society. According to those who level the charge, such sectarians are so preoccupied with their own identity that they insulate themselves from other "less provincial" currents of thought and life.

> Sectarianism in theology and ethics becomes a seductive temptation. Religiously and theologically it provides Christians with a clear distinctiveness from others in beliefs; morally it provides distinctiveness in behavior. It ensures a clear identity which frees persons from ambiguity and uncertainty, but it isolates Christianity from taking seriously the wider world of science and culture and limits the participation of Christians in the ambiguities of moral and social life in the patterns of interdependence in the world (Gustafson 1985:84).

Gustafson's comments about "the wider world of science and culture" point to a closely related assumption. Critics assume not only the priority of a more universal community but also that such a community is made possible by some overarching, context-independent form of rationality that underwrites a more global and less provincial conversation. "Sectarians" are those who choose not to participate in this conversation on its own terms because they sense something important is lost in doing so — notably, the particular Christian shape of their convictions, practices, and narratives. For example, if Christians want to participate in the societal conversation about ethics, they are told that they should bracket their particular convictions and stories and enter into the arena where decisions are evaluated on the basis of an ostensibly neutral rationality. At the very least, they are told, they should argue for their ethical positions not on the basis of their particular confessions of faith, but on grounds that will seem justifiable to Christian and non-Christian alike.

> No one doubts the importance of decision in Ethics, or the significance of confessions in the households of faith, but the critical questions have to do with whether there are *warrants* for the decisions we have to make, whether there is *good reason* for making the decisions we do, and whether there are *justifiable grounds* for identifying some things that *we all* ought to decide for or against (Stackhouse 1987:13; emphasis added).

Those who hold such a position seem to believe that what counts for warrants, good reasons, and justifiable grounds can be separated from the particularities of convictions, practices, and narratives. But such assumptions have been radically called into question both by those who have argued that foundationalist epistemologies are seriously flawed and by those who have criticized ahistorical notions of reason (MacIntyre 1988). Said another way, those who stress notions of universal community and rationality tend to downplay if not completely ignore the ways in which their own commitments and convictions have been shaped by *particular* communities and traditions (academic and otherwise). As a result, these critics tend to ignore the no-less-provincial character of their own convictions, narratives, and practices.

We see the link most clearly between the assumptions about universal human community and rationality when sectarians are rebuked for ignoring their responsibility to this wider human community. When Christians respond by insisting that their responsibility to this wider world is primarily one of service and witness, the typical rejoinder is that responsible Christian witness cannot take place unless Christians are willing to bracket their particularities and engage in the debate on more universal, less provincial terms. Hence, Christians are regularly reminded that if they desire their witness to be effective, they must be willing to translate their peculiarly Christian convictions into a more universal language. The question is always cast in terms of whether or not Christians will participate in the liberal democratic conversation/dialogue on its own terms. If they will not, insisting that their way of life cannot be rightly understood apart from the particularities of their convictions and narratives, then they are often criticized for being sectarian. One such critic helpfully articulates what he takes to be the dangers inherent in such sectarian attitudes:

> "Sectarianism," in its usual sense, entails the impossibility of any rational dialogue with those outside the "sect," on the grounds that their epistemically and morally central convictions are corrupt and diametrically opposed to those of "insiders." Attempts at forging a consensus would, then, be not merely futile but dangerous, since arguing the point on "their" terms would only serve to undermine "ours." Sectarians are then faced with the options of either proclaiming their confession to "the world" and having it fall upon deaf ears, or articulating only among themselves the truth to which they bear witness. Surely this is not a particularly comforting situation. This sort of sectarianism inevitably falls back on fideism and voluntarism.... It is an "in-house" affair,

culturally marginal, and worst of all, lacking in any
sort of robust rationality (Quirk 1987:81–82).

This critic's use of "insider" and "outsider" language points
to one of the most damning charges against and deepest
assumptions about sectarians — that they insulate themselves from critique and correction. I will deal at length
with this assumption later in this chapter. Two other points,
however, are germane at this juncture. First, before the
distinction made above between "fideism" and "robust rationality" can be made to do any work, an important though
debatable epistemological assumption must be securely in
place. One must presuppose that appeals to faith or trust
and appeals to reason are at odds with each other as humans seek knowledge. But the assumption that trust and
reason are contradictory epistemological postures has been
radically called into question in all arenas of human inquiry,
including math and science.[23] Rather than viewing faith or
trust as opposed to reason, more and more people are coming to see that all knowledge is rooted in convictions and
commitments of trust. In short, a consensus is emerging
that Augustine may well have been right when he offered
his famous slogan, *credo ut intelligam* — I believe in order to
know (Newbigin 1995).

Second, it is hardly self-evident that sectarians, who refuse to adopt a putatively less parochial standpoint, must
choose between speaking their own language to a world
that remains deaf to it and speaking only to themselves.
Indeed, one wonders if the critic above believes it is self-
evident because he regards it as tautological; that is, sectarians simply are those who, appearances to the contrary,
are speaking only to themselves. But such circular reason-
ing has a kind of self-perpetuating effect. In other words,

what seems to make sectarians "sectarian" is that they have only these two options available. If this indeed is the working assumption, then it suggests that coming up with other options might very well call into question their sectarian status.

What might such options look like? First, we should note that the two options offered are the only ones available only so long as we also assume that the initial or primary point of contact between the Christian community and "the wider society" is the liberal democratic discourse or conversation.[24] But why must this dialogue, carried on at a high level of generality and abstraction, be the primary point of contact? In other words, why must the point of contact be something like a theory of justice or a theory of the human person? Why couldn't the day-to-day contact with the lives of Christians, their living and embodied witness, serve as a point of contact? Of course, if the church *has* no distinctive, embodied witness, that is certainly a problem, but that is quite a different issue. The question right now concerns why the deck seems to be stacked such that even if the church *had* such an embodied witness it would count for little or nothing. An appeal to such an embodied witness will not eliminate, of course, the need for some form of dialogue or conversation. Nevertheless, insisting that such witness is central to the life and mission of the church might serve as a reminder that the liberal democratic model of dialogue, when it becomes an end in itself, can seduce the church into believing that its primary concern with regard to witness is to find new and effective ways of translating a disembodied message.[25]

Many thinkers in our postmodern era have raised serious questions about the wisdom of the West's penchant for making abstract notions of universality and rationality the linchpin of its thinking and acting. Once such notions are rendered suspect, much of the sting of being labeled a sectarian is lost, because now the focus shifts inexorably to the crucial role in human affairs played by the particular, the local, and the contingent (Toulmin 1990).

Culture as Monolithic

In ways closely related to the above discussion, those who level the charge of sectarianism routinely speak as if culture is a monolithic entity. This central assumption largely fuels the accusation of global withdrawal. Sectarians are not merely castigated for their refusal to participate in particular cultural activities; in addition, they are commonly accused of withdrawing from some monolithic entity called "culture." This problematic use of the concept "culture" is critical to the thesis of H. Richard Niebuhr's highly influential work:

> What we have in view when we deal with Christ and culture is that total process of human activity and that total result of such activity to which now the name *culture*, now the name *civilization*, is applied in common speech. Culture is the "artificial, secondary environment" which man superimposes on the natural. It comprises language, habits, ideas, beliefs, customs, social organization, inherited artifacts, technical processes, and values. This "social heritage," this "reality sui generis," which the New Testament writers frequently had in mind when they spoke of "the world," which is represented in many forms but to which Christians like other men are inevitably subject, is what we mean when we speak of culture (1951:32).

Niebuhr's typology assumes that culture is monolithic: all five responses treat culture as if it presents itself as a single totality. Whether Niebuhr writes of Christ "against," "of," or "above" culture, of Christ and culture in paradox, or of Christ as transformer of culture, he writes as if this entity called "culture" is a single undifferentiated entity. Thus, when Niebuhr establishes at the very beginning of his project the character of the "enduring problem," he writes: "It is not essentially the problem of Christianity and civilization; for Christianity, whether defined as church, creed, ethics, or movement of thought, itself moves between the poles of Christ and culture. The relation of these two authorities constitutes the problem" (:11). To be fair, Niebuhr's usage reflects attitudes about "culture" and "civilization" common for his day.[26] Moreover, he does occasionally hint that culture may not be as monolithic as his typology suggests. Nevertheless, Niebuhr reins in this potentially troubling insight by locating it within his broader discussion of "pluralism." Not surprisingly, the pluralism Niebuhr discusses is not so much a pluralism of cultures within a given society but a pluralism of "values" within that culture.

The values we seek in our societies and find represented in their institutional behavior are many, disparate, and often incomparable, so that these societies are always involved in a more or less laborious effort to hold together in tolerable conflict the many efforts of many men in many groups to achieve and conserve many goods. The cultures are forever seeking to combine peace with prosperity, justice with order, freedom with welfare, truth with beauty, scientific truth with moral good, technical proficiency with practical wisdom, holiness with life, and all these with all the rest.

Among the many values the kingdom of God may be included — though scarcely as the one pearl of great price. Jesus Christ and God the Father, the gospel, the church, and eternal life may find places in *the cultural complex*, but only as elements in the great pluralism.

These are some of the obvious characteristics of *that culture* which lays its claim on every Christian, and under the authority of which he also lives when he lives under the authority of Jesus Christ (:38–39; emphasis added).[27]

According to Niebuhr, sectarians represent the "Christ against Culture" type. These Christians believe that the two poles of "Christ" and "culture" are diametrically opposed: "Whatever may be the customs of the society in which the Christian lives, and whatever the human achievements it conserves, Christ is seen as opposed to them, so that he confronts men with the challenge of an 'either-or' decision" (:40). Moreover, because such sectarians are said to reject something called "culture" *in toto*, they are often accused of lapsing into some form of gnosticism that ultimately denies the goodness of creation and the possibility of the Incarnation. Again, Niebuhr is representative, especially in his bid to paint the sectarians as extremists:

The *extreme temptation* the *radicals* meet when they deal with these questions is that of converting their ethical dualism into an ontological bifurcation of reality. *Their rejection of culture* is easily combined with a suspicion of nature and nature's God. . . . At the edges of the *radical* movement the Manichean heresy is always developing (:81; emphasis added).[28]

But neither the Christian doctrine of creation nor of the Incarnation offers any kind of blanket approval to some monolithic entity called "culture." Instead, Christian doctrine affirms that humans live in a corrupt and fragmented world that still finds itself in the grip of the principalities and powers. The so-called sectarians step into such a setting to offer an embodied witness that Jesus, not the principalities and powers, is Lord. This is in contrast to those who, on the basis of faith in an abstraction called "the goodness of creation," feel the need to affirm something called "culture" with little or no attempt at discrimination or discernment on the basis of the Lordship of Christ. What cannot be forgotten is that the Son, who is also active in creation, calls for radical obedience and discipleship. One cannot pit the creator against the redeemer. Thus, the tendency to speak of culture as if it were a monolithic entity itself creates several problems, not the least of which is that it muffles the clear note within the Christian traditions that humans live in a created, though fallen, world. It is the fallen character of creation that requires discernment and judgment regarding all aspects of human cultures, though the need for such discernment is neither acknowledged nor encouraged by Niebuhr's typology. In fact, it is Niebuhr's monolithic understanding of culture that makes it possible for him to create a type ("Christ against culture") composed of those who reject the entire culture (difficult as that is to imagine in either theory or practice). Such a typology misrepresents those Christians who engage in ongoing practices of discernment to determine in which cultural activities they may participate and in which ones they should not.

If one begins with a less monolithic understanding of culture — something more modest than equating culture with civilization — questions emerge other than the ones on which Niebuhr focused.[29] For example, a different set of issues emerges if one begins with a comment by Raymond Williams, who suggests that culture is a "signifying system through which necessarily (though among other means) a social order is communicated, reproduced, experienced and explored" (1982:13). Such a starting point reminds us that within a given society, particularly one as expansive as the United States, there are multiple signifying systems and concomitant practices that inevitably attempt, more or less successfully, to reproduce a social order commensurate with that signifying system. Each of these cultures is minimally an embodied argument about what reality is like and the place of humans beings within it.

When any given society contains a multiplicity of cultures (understood as embodied and instituted signifying systems), certain questions are bound to arise, such as whether and how one culture should (or even can) be compared with another. Is there some "cultureless" position from which to judge? Or is every judgment about one culture inevitably based on the central and operative convictions of another? If we likely find ourselves in the latter position, then it is harder to make sense of the charge, routinely aimed at sectarians, that they attempt "to withdraw from culture and to give up all responsibility for the world" (Niebuhr 1951:57). As Yoder rightly notes, when Niebuhr uses the language of culture in this way, it is difficult to see how he can mean anything more than "the majority position of a given society" (1996:56).[30] But if this is so, then Niebuhr has, by means of his assumption of a monolithic culture, papered over what would be better characterized as a clash of competing cultures. Naming it as a clash of cultures encourages us to ask further questions, such as: What distinguishes one culture from another? Can one be a participant in more than one? If so, how are the inevitable tensions that arise from multiple memberships to be nego-tiated? All of these questions and more are left unanswered, even unasked, as long as culture is viewed as monolithic and those who "withdraw" from it are casually dismissed as irresponsible sectarians.

Beginning with a less monolithic view of culture will ob-viously not resolve all the problems with which the churches in contemporary societies are faced; enormous tensions and difficult judgments will still need to be made. But as Yoder rightly suggests, redescribing the situation would likely make a considerable difference in how we name "the problem":

> The tension will not be between a global reality called "culture" on one side and an absolute spiritual distance called "Christ" (or "monotheism") on the other side, but rather between a group of people defined by a commitment to Christ seeking cultural expression of that commitment (on one hand) and (on the other) a group or groups of other people expressing culturally other values which are independent of or contradic-tory to such a confession. This latter group is what the New Testament calls "the world" (1996:74).

Once the so-called sectarians are rescued from having to reject all of culture in principle, they can likewise be res-cued from the charge of failing to be consistent in their practice. That is, once we allow that these Christians never insisted that human cultural embodiment could or should be altogether avoided (indeed, quite the contrary), we need not fault them (as Niebuhr does) for failing to live up to that ideal. Certainly, most sectarians have not thought it necessary to reject all language, agriculture, the arts, struggles for social justice, medicine, or technology, to name only a few cultural arenas where spiritual discernment, not rejection *in toto,* is called for. I will return to the important role of discernment in the Christian community in the final chapter.

The Shape of "Politics" as Given

A closely related set of assumptions concerns the status of "politics." Those who level the charge of sectarianism often imply that anything less than full and enthusiastic participation in this one important, though hardly all-encompassing, arena of society amounts to withdrawal from all aspects of cultural life. Hence, those who withdraw from politics as normally construed, especially as it concerns the necessary use of violence, are considered sectarian. For example, Yoder notes how Niebuhr assumes an

> unquestioning commitment to the necessity of managing society from the top and his identification of political control with "culture." Tolstoy was in favor of story-telling, the novel, the folk tale, the arts, the family, the village, the school, the restoration of peasant crafts, and heavy labor in the fields, but because he rejected the *sword* he is pigeonholed as a radical anticulturalist. Thus government becomes exemplary for all of culture (:66).

This easy reduction of all culture to politics is particularly troubling when politics is itself reduced to the territorial disputes of nation-states or the official business of the legislative branches of governments. This view of politics abandons the broader and more classical view of politics as the art of ordering human social life in favor of a more circumscribed understanding that limits politics to the official actions of governments.[31] Charging Christians who "withdraw" from this more circumscribed arena with being sectarian only makes sense if one makes a further assumption. Before the charge can carry any weight, those who level it must demonstrate that the arena of public policy as normally understood is unquestionably the only way (or at least the most important way) in which real differences are made in how people order their lives together as communities. Yet such an argument is rarely offered. Instead, critics merely assume that the only legitimate and truly responsible way to engage and transform society is to participate in this relatively circumscribed activity that the West has come to call "politics." Such unquestioned assumptions about the nature of politics make it possible for a reputable scholar like Peter Kaufman to begin an article on "sectarian Protestantism" with the following observation: "Most would agree that early Christian piety was apolitical. 'Nations' might reawaken and carve up idiosyncratically the territories accumulated by Rome, but the new religion was principally concerned with an everlasting kingdom" (1982:75). Perhaps it is telling that Kaufman recognizes the dangers of anachronistically projecting the notion of "nations" back into the first century, but he has no such qualms with equating "politics" with the carving up of territories. Why are such political practices given a privileged position such that less than wholehearted participation in them makes one "apolitical"? To assume that anyone who is disinterested in the carving up of territories is automatically disinterested in how human communities order their lives together appears no less narrow or sectarian. Thus, as Walter Brueggemann suggests, the empire can itself be sectarian.

We are not accustomed to thinking of the voice of the empire as a sectarian voice. But so it is when it serves only a narrow interest. *Empire as sect* is a theme worth pursuing in our own situation because it may be suggested that the voice of American power, for example, claims to be the voice of general well-being and may in a number of cases be only the voice of a narrow range of economic and political interest. The ideological guise is effective if large numbers of people can be kept from noticing the narrow base of real interest (1985:22–23).

Behind the charge of sectarian withdrawal, therefore, lurks a certain unexamined view of what counts for "real" politics, a particular view of politics and public policy that is simply and unproblematically given. Thus, when theologian Ronald Thiemann articulates his agenda for constructing a "public theology," what makes his project intelligible (and presumably necessary) is the assumption that the positions he labels "sectarian" are less political, less engaged in the public arena.

Neither the politicization of worship nor its sectarian separation from public life will suffice in our current situation. We must engage in a basic rethinking of the very categories by which we understand the church's relation to public life. We must find a middle way between the reduction of the Christian gospel to a program of political action and the isolation of that gospel from all political engagement (1991:114).

Ironically, Thiemann himself fails to rethink "the very categories by which we understand the church's relation to public life"; he simply reinscribes them and then looks for some kind of middle ground. For example, he leaves unexamined the categories of "sectarian," "public life," "political action," and "political engagement." Thiemann is right that these categories and their givenness is a problem; unfortunately he offers no help in moving beyond them. To see the constricted view of politics with which most people operate, consider the following example. If Christians lobby Congress to restrict the amount of violence on television, this is considered "real political action." If Christians put their television sets in the closet, however, this is considered a private matter, a personal lifestyle choice, a simple apolitical preference. But certainly if all people who regard themselves as Christians did the latter, this action would have a sizable impact on the social order we call the United States of America. Isn't such ordering of the social the traditional concern of politics?

This suggests that as long as the realm of politics is defined in such a constricted sense, what will count as legitimate participation in such a realm will likewise be constricted. Thus, it is only because such a view of politics is in place that certain Christians can be faulted for preserving their distinct identity by sacrificing full participation in politics (Gustafson 1985:94). But why should maintaining one's Christian identity and participating in politics be pitted against each other? This only follows if one has already decided what is going to count for political participation in a given public arena and what rules will govern it. As Yoder helpfully reminds us, "there is no 'public' that is not just another province" (1984:40). This is why several Christian thinkers have suggested that few entities exhibit a more sectarian, a more provincial, a more tribal posture than the empire or nation-state.

We reject the charge of tribalism, particularly from those whose theologies serve to buttress the most nefarious brand of tribalism of all — the omnipotent state. The church is the one political entity in our culture that is global, transnational, transcultural. Tribalism is not the church determined to serve God rather than Caesar. Tribalism is the United States of America, which sets up artificial boundaries and defends them with murderous intensity. And the tribalism of nations occurs most viciously in the absence of a church able to say and show, in its life together, that God, not nations, rules the world (Hauerwas and Willimon 1989:42–43).

A view of the church that calls the church to challenge the idolatry of the nation-state is difficult to establish or sustain in Western cultures. Part of the reason, as will be discussed in the next section, concerns the widespread agreement in Western cultures about the proper bounds of "religion." Part of the grammar of "religion" in Western cultures is that it is an intellectual/moral system that is private and apolitical. If adherents of a particular "religion" want to bring their convictions into the public/political arena, they must be willing to translate them into the cultural vernacular of the day. But as John Milbank reminds us, the Christian faith is not a world-view, a system of intellectual propositions whose mere acceptance thereby differentiates Christian from non-Christian.

It is apparent that at least as important a site of uniqueness is the ecclesial project itself; no other religious community comprehends itself (in theory) as an international society, independent of political regimes and legal codes, including as equal members (in some sense) men, women, and children, without regard to social class and committed to the realization, within this society, of perfect mutual acceptance and cooperative interaction (1990a:179).

A community that embodied such a vision could hardly be considered narrow or provincial. Indeed, what makes such a vision anything but sectarian is that it radically calls into question the reigning assumptions not only about what counts for "politics," but also about what counts for "religion." With this in mind, we turn to the assumptions undergirding this latter concept.

The Shape of "Religion" as Given

Charges of sectarianism are rooted not only in a certain view of "politics," but also in a certain view of "religion." In fact, these two sets of presuppositions are intimately related. What is thought to count as a legitimate religion (and by extension, therefore, what is thought to count as deviancy with regards to religion — i.e., sectarianism) is inextricably bound up in contemporary Western societies with certain notions of politics. Indeed, Talal Asad argues not only that modernity created "religion," but also that this creation was part and parcel of the rise of the modern state:

Historians of seventeenth- and eighteenth-century Europe have begun to recount how the constitution of the modern state required the forcible redefinition of religion as belief, and of religious belief, sentiment, and identity as personal matters that belong to the newly emerging space of private (as opposed to public) life.... Scholars are now more aware that religious toleration was a political means to the formation of the strong state power that emerged from the sectarian wars of the sixteenth and seventeenth centuries rather than the gift of a benign intention to defend pluralism (1993:205–06; cf. Cavanaugh 1995).

Asad reminds us how relatively recently the West has come to view religion as a sphere whose defining feature is a set of beliefs that are understood to be separable from actions. With the rise of the constitutional state came the "construction of religion as a new historical object: anchored in personal experience, expressible as belief statements, dependent on private institutions, and practiced in one's spare time." And as Asad goes on to insist, this construction of religion ensured that religion was regarded "as *inessential* to our common politics, economy, science, and morality" (:207). Not surprisingly, this strong distinction between private belief and public action remains central to many Western societies' understandings of religion. In the United States, for example, this distinction underwrites many interpretations of the First Amendment. In *Cantwell* v. *Connecticut* (1940), the Supreme Court wrote: "The First Amendment embraces two concepts — freedom to believe and freedom to act. The first is absolute but, in the nature of things, the second cannot be. Conduct remains subject to regulation for the protection of society" (Flowers 1994:23).

Most people would agree that any social order will find it necessary to regulate conduct. What is bothersome is the assumption that belief can be divorced from action. Such a view limits belief almost entirely to the cognitive realm. With this view of belief, it makes sense to tell anarchists that they can believe whatever they like about the superiority of anarchy as long as they do not intend to act on those beliefs. But if these beliefs are not merely intellectual postures, but deeply held convictions, then it seems harder to understand what sense it would make to tell people that they were free to hold certain convictions as long as they did not intend to act on them. Does it make sense to say: "I have a deeply held conviction that Jesus Christ is Lord of all of life, but I have no intention of acting on that conviction"? Most people would understandably regard not acting on a deeply held conviction as *prima facie* evidence that one does not hold it (or that one does not hold it as "deeply" as one supposes). Thus, if social orders must regulate certain actions (and it seems obvious that they must), then it would seem more honest if they would also admit that they must regulate certain beliefs or convictions as well. This would helpfully discourage us from driving a wedge between our private beliefs and public actions.

Ironically, the so-called sectarians are often the ones who violate the sacrosanct boundaries between private belief and public action, convicted as they are that their entire lives, not merely some private sphere, must be imbued with their "religious" convictions. Said differently, those labeled sectarians are not those people who withdraw from the public or political. Rather, they are those people who refuse to operate with two distinct sets of convictions — one "religious" set that informs their private devotion and one "political" set that shapes their public actions. As a result, so-called sects (and the "fanatics" that comprise them) almost always embody a less fragmented (and therefore more "totalizing") vision that threatens securely circumscribed notions of religion. It is telling that most persons in the United States are much less suspicious of "fans" (probably a shortened form of "fanatic") of college football than they are of so-called religious fanatics. In other words, to order one's entire identity and waking life around one's loyalty to a group of late-adolescents who fight over a 100–yard stretch of real estate each Saturday afternoon in autumn is perhaps slightly eccentric, but certainly understandable and acceptable. However, to order one's entire identity and waking life around one's allegiance to Jesus Christ as Lord of the cosmos and to his church is fanatical and downright dangerous. Such groups clearly overstep the bounds of Western respectability and propriety. Such groups clearly need to be taught moderation, which in matters of "religion" means making sure that these convictions and practices remain subordinate to other more dominant cultural convictions and practices.

A more sympathetic understanding of those groups labeled as sects would be to regard them as embodied arguments against the conventional "compartmentalization of religion," a phrase whose redundancy is now evident. Unfortunately, this compartmentalization is itself part of the very logic, or "grammar," of the concept of religion in modern Western cultures.[32] Those labeled sectarians challenge this received notion by attempting to embody a social alternative where Christian convictions and practices are not relegated to the periphery.

Once a healthy suspicion of Western understandings of "religion" has been established, we may turn our attention once again to that discipline where the language of sect is most at home — the sociology of religion. In the first chapter I suggested that sociology is never purely descriptive. We are now in a position to see this point more clearly. If one of the primary defining features of sectarianism is deviancy from the norm, then the circular nature of sect identification becomes apparent. That is, one cannot identify something as deviant without simultaneously defining something as normative. Thus, when sociologists of religion search for common functions of sects, they usually find them only by assuming that certain dominant patterns of religiosity in a given society are normative. Even though they purport to be only describing these patterns, they are always evaluating them as well by granting a certain legitimacy to those positions identified as normative and denying such legitimacy to those deemed deviant. This becomes clear in Wilson's comments on the functional essence of sects:

> It is evident, both from the large numbers of sects which have arisen in certain periods of history, and from their diversity, that the common functions of sects for their members can be expressed in only the most general terms. But one of these functions has obviously been the heightened sense of commitment and distinctiveness which sectarianism implies. The members of the major Churches or denominations are often indistinguishable from one another in most of their secular concerns. They tend to be more characterized by their occupation, their education, or by purely personal dispositions than by their religious affiliation. But the sectarian is almost always conspicuous by virtue of his religious commitment. Whatever activity he is engaged in, the fact that a man is one of Jehovah's Witnesses, or a Christadelphian, or even a Quaker, tends to become evident sooner rather than later. . . . In some European countries those religious institutions which once boasted the name and the reality of Churches are, with secularization, faced with being reduced to the status of sects; that is to say, of being reduced to relatively small, heterodox groups who believe and practice things which are alien to the

majority. They differ from sects, however, in lacking the intensity of commitment (1966:182, 223).

Wilson's observations appear to be purely descriptive: a group with a heightened sense of commitment and distinctiveness is called a sect. But clearly he takes as normative the desire both to blend into the cultural landscape and to evade intense commitment. Even if sociologists mean no harm by describing certain groups as sects, certainly such usage reinforces the normative status of those not so identified. In other words, by regarding certain models of the church as normative, sociologists have indeed taken sides by granting continued legitimacy to these "normative" models and denying it to those identified as sects. For example, Christians who believe they are called to embody a contrast-society must be willing to make discernments in particular times and places about whether, how, and to what extent they should be distinguishable from the wider society, given their particular discernments about the character of that wider society. Granted, most Christians in the West do not currently operate with such a view of the church. But to determine ahead of time that exercising such discernment earns one the label of "sectarian" is to make (perhaps unwittingly) such theological discernment peripheral to what it means to be the church by labeling it as somehow deviant.

No less disturbing are the ways sociologists routinely account for sectarian allegiances by attributing them to their "real" (nontheological) origins. For example, sociologists of religion often describe the adherents of sects as somehow alienated from mainstream society. This alienation is usually characterized as social, cultural, or economic in nature. Although many sociologists avoid explicitly claiming that these factors are the only ones involved, too often the impression given is that the proffered sociological explanation is the real reason why something happened. For example, Wilson encourages us to

> acknowledge the extent to which Niebuhr's insight into the social basis of denominationalism was warranted. New religious movements are frequently vehicles for sections of society which are otherwise unaccommodated socially and religiously. When the productive relations of a society are changing, new groups of men find some need for a reinterpretation of their position. New classes seek then their own transcendental justification, and so all the more vigorously for being excluded from the existing distribution of social honour and religious sanctity (:201).

Even though Wilson appears to be acknowledging both social and religious factors, it turns out that the social factors are the real impetus for new religious movements whereas the religious factors are best understood as attempts at "transcendental justification." In a similar fashion, the missiologist Nils Bloch-Hoell insists that protest movements within Christianity have both religious and sociological roots; however, his way of making this point tends to privilege sociological explanations: "As Ernst Troeltsch among others has pointed out, the adherents of enthusiasts like Thomas Müntzer and Jan van Leyden came mainly from the lower strata of society. What the radical left wing of Protestants believed to be pure religious protest was to a great extent motivated and modelled by sociological factors" (1978:24). Here the rhetoric of "pure religious protest" is based on modern conceptions of religion, that assume that economic and religious matters can be neatly separated. The assumption is of an autonomous social or economic sphere that actually shapes the life and actions of people, whereas the religious or theological sphere merely offers thinly veiled justifications.

Sociologists of religion, like all people, operate with numerous presuppositions. Many of these assumptions are widely acknowledged as being antitheological in character. Bryan Wilson, for example, has stated that "the founders of sociology, Auguste Comte and, in some measure, his immediate predecessor, Henri Saint-Simon, saw the new science, which Comte designated 'sociology,' as a replacement of the theological interpretation of social phenomena" (1982:1). Or as Milbank has argued, sociology reinforces a view of the world that is not so much antitheological in character as it is a view of the world that competes with theological views, and is, therefore, itself a kind of "faith."[33] In other words, by creating an ostensibly autonomous realm called "the social," sociology claims to explain what is *really* going on in the world without recourse to theological interpretation. So, for example, when sociologists claim that sectarian movements often arise among the lower strata of society, this is taken as evidence that the origins of these movements are social or economic rather than religious or theological. By suggesting that such movements are unaware of their true origins, these sorts of explanations make it easier for protest and reform movements to be casually dismissed. Why should such movements be taken seriously theologically, once it has been demonstrated that the real basis for such protest is not theological but economic? That the arguments of sociologists sound reasonable to many of us only suggests how deeply we have bought into modern conceptions of religion — conceptions that have stripped Christian faith and practice of any social or economic content of its own.

Let us revisit the sociological explanation of sect development as rooted in social and economic alienation and consider whether there might not be reasons internal to the logic of Christianity that might account for this sociological evidence. The New Testament has often been read as suggesting that people are more receptive to the claims of the gospel when they *are* alienated from the centers of power, wealth, and prestige (Matt. 19:16–30; Luke 12:13–34; 16:19–31; 1 Cor. 3:18–23). Indeed, Jesus intimates on several occasions that being privy to power and wealth makes it extremely difficult to hear the gospel as good news. Such remarks remind us that our tendency to drive a wedge between theological explanations and economic or social ones is a relatively recent habit of thought.[34] At the very least, therefore, the observation that a sect draws a large part of its constituency from certain strata of society cannot necessarily be viewed as evidence that the "real" origins of the sect are not theological.

This brief detour through the sociology of religion has been necessary in order to underscore the way in which certain understandings of "religion" have shaped and continue to shape discussions of sectarianism. This foray suggests that a renarrating of so-called sociological evidence might have important missiological implications in the West. For example, the difficulties felt by so many today in establishing a stable sense of identity might provide new opportunities for presenting the radical claims of the Lordship of Christ. Those people who have no satisfying way of establishing their identity might be surprisingly receptive to the comprehensive reordering of life that becoming a disciple of Jesus Christ entails. Their being receptive, however, would not necessarily give credence to those sociological accounts that make the rise of sectarian groups a reaction to that which is more fundamental, such as social instability.[35] Rather than claiming that social turmoil *causes* the rise of protest or reform movements, we might think of such social unrest as producing the social and cultural space for the claims of such movements to appear plausible in ways that are difficult when people are comfortably sleepwalking through social bliss and stability.

Insulation from Critique[36]

The final set of presuppositions that underwrite the charge of sectarianism concerns the way in which so-called sectarian models seemingly insulate the church from critique. Some schismatic groups imply that they alone possess the truth, lending credibility to the fear that such groups are so insulated that they deny both the possibility and desirability of learning from anyone outside their group (including other professed Christians). But when the charge of sectarianism is hurled in the current debates, these schismatics are not normally the intended targets. Instead, the target is usually the so-called postliberals, whose particularist understanding of the church seems quite amenable to those who believe the church is called to be a contrast-society.[37]

As noted earlier, some of the most powerful insights of the postliberal scheme stem from its suggestion that we should think of religions as languages, and doctrine as their grammars. Yet it is precisely at this point that postliberalism's critics become worried. Postliberalism appears to grant "religious" ways of construing the world no less legitimacy and authority than other ways of construing it, such as the "scientific." Indeed, postliberalism encourages Christians to grant the biblical narrative supreme importance as their central and ultimately defining narrative. Critics worry that such a position implies that these are just *different* ways of looking at the world, with no neutral or disinterested way to adjudicate disagreements among them. The result, according to the critics, is that each view becomes self-enclosed and self-justifying, with no possibility of critique from anything outside it. As James Gustafson writes:

> The incommensurability of scientific and religious language means that the same person and communities will have two very different ways of construing the reality of life in the world side by side. From this perspective of the division of languages, one has no bearing upon the other. Theology and the morality of the Christian community necessarily become what I have called sectarian.... It is difficult to see how one can make any critique of the tradition, internal or external.... Doctrine becomes ideology. It isolates theology from any correction by other modes of construing reality (1985:85–86).

These are obviously serious charges that need to be examined closely. Are the critics correct? Before we can decide, we need to examine the presuppositions that inform these charges.

To begin, the charge contains within it two separate and seemingly quite different accusations. First, postliberal theology is said to construe the world and the Christian faith in a way that insulates its construals from *any* external criticism. We might call this the impulse to isolationism; here the Christian faith is insulated from critique because it is *sealed off* from other forms of discourse. Second, there is the charge that postliberal theology so privileges Christian narratives that all other narratives and explanatory schemes are subordinated to it. We might call this the impulse to imperialism; here the Christian faith is insulated from critique because its story is already considered superior to other narratives and therefore not open to correction by them.[38] Although these two charges are clearly related, it may be helpful to distinguish them as we proceed to examine the presuppositions underlying them.

The Impulse to Isolationism

First, critics seem to assume as normative the modern fragmentation of life into autonomous spheres (such as the religious or political or medical), each with its own discourse and inner logic. When contemporary life requires people to move in and out of several different spheres or several different communities organized around those spheres, they are expected to submit to the dominant discourses, practices, and authorities of those spheres. If Christians are guided by or presume to speak on the basis of their faith about something that ostensibly belongs to another sphere, they are criticized for being narrow or sectarian. To refuse to take into account that sphere's discourse and practice is to lapse into sectarianism by insulating the Christian faith from broader views or important critiques that those spheres might offer. Gustafson, for example, claims that the assumption that underwrites postliberal theology and ethics

> breaks on the rocks of the fact that Christians do (and ought to) participate in their professions, their political communities and other aspects of the social order. Their moral lives are not confined to some Christian community; they take place where choices have to be made that are not only moral but economic, political, medical and so forth. If the test of the morality

> of Christians becomes its conformity to some version
> of the imitation of Christ, or some fidelity to the
> meaning of the Biblical narratives, either Christians
> are put into positions of intense inner conflict or they
> must withdraw from participation in any structures
> which would presumably compromise their fidelity to
> Jesus. . . . Even descriptively the sociological assump-
> tion of this is false. Christians, whether they choose
> to or not, are members of, and make choices in, other
> social communities (1985:91–92).

If the contours of community are defined by particular
convictions, practices, and narratives, along with our loyalty to them, then Gustafson is right: we all likely find
ourselves in multiple communities. But surely Christians
are not the only ones who find themselves trying to ne-
gotiate competing narratives and practices (and therefore
communities). For example, how should we conceive the
relationship between the narratives that shape our legal system (which are necessarily rooted in notions of personal
responsibility) and those that are being told more frequently
in scientific journals (which often speak primarily in terms
of brain chemistry)? *Must* there be some neutral way to
adjudicate the competing claims made by these two different narratives? It seems possible that these narratives, along
with their concomitant practices and convictions, might
represent radically different (and potentially contradictory)
visions of what it means to be human.

This leads us to a second presupposition. Critics of
postliberalism insist that there really is only one viable so-
lution to the problem of competing narratives: there simply
must be some reasonable way to adjudicate these competing
claims on our lives. Gustafson writes:

Sectarians might admit that the Christian community does not live in a cultural ghetto, but go on to propose that there are double, triple, or quadruple truths which are incommensurable with each other. Christians live in separable communities each with its own language. This seems to me to create problems of moral and intellectual integrity for Christians; they would have to interpret and explain the same events in different ways as they left the doors of the Church and went home to read the newspapers, the scientific journals, or watch television (1985:91).

Part of the problem is that Gustafson seems to beg the question of what the relationship among these multiple commitments and narratives ought to be. He simply assumes, as an heir of modernity, that these autonomous spheres ought to remain autonomous, except that the Christian community ought to be open to correction from other disciplines when it deals with matters that are the province of one of these other autonomous spheres. Moreover, Gustafson's talk of "correction" earlier seems to assume that competing discourses share enough in common for correction to take place. But it is not at all clear that such commonalties are always in place. Even if it were, however, it is not clear that Gustafson is advocating mutual correction. Instead, Gustafson wants Christian discourse to be corrected by ostensibly more authoritative discourses. To see this more clearly, one need only ask whether he expects politics, economics, medicine, and morality to be "corrected" by Christian theology, or whether this corrective process runs only one way.

Finally, the charge of isolationism assumes that the language of internal and external is unproblematic. Indeed, at times the critics write as if this distinction is empirical. Over and over again they insist that the Christian faith must remain open to "external" criticism; but such language is quite slippery. As Stanley Fish has helpfully pointed out, we tend to assume that "the distinction between outside and inside is empirical and absolute, whereas in fact it is an interpretive distinction between realms that are interdependent rather than discrete" (1989:148). Said differently, the line between internal and external is never permanently fixed, because there is always the possibility that what is external will become internal. What makes this an *interpretive* distinction is that such a shift always entails the redrawing of the lines from the *inside*. For example, when the early Jewish followers of Jesus were confronted with the mission to the Gentiles, they were willing to rethink the boundaries of the people of God at least partly because they were capable of conceptualizing this change *from the inside*. When the Council of Jerusalem met, as recorded in Acts 15, they were well aware that including the Gentiles would amount to a momentous change. But the reasons the Council gives for justifying this change do not come from outside the Jewish heritage, even if the impetus for the change might have been. Continuity with the old is maintained both by arguing for this change on the basis of Scripture (Amos 9:11–12) and by insisting that the Gentiles respect those prohibitions that were enjoined even of non-Israelite strangers (cf. Lev. 17:8–9, 12, 14–15; 18:16–18).[39] Thus the Council of Jerusalem is much like the scribe to whom Jesus alludes: the Council brings out of its treasure what is old and what is new (Matt 13:52). This seems to confirm Fish's point: "When the community is persuaded (by arguments that rely on assumptions not at the moment being challenged) that its project requires the taking into account of what had hitherto been considered beside the point or essential only to someone else's point — the boundaries of outside/inside will have been redrawn, and redrawn from the inside" (:148). It seems to me that much of the use of the Old Testament in the New could be profitably understood in such terms.

What critics of postliberalism seem to overlook is that the Christian faith, like all frameworks, includes a mechanism for responding to criticism and making judgments about change. Furthermore, some critics of postliberalism seem to confuse the *impetus* for change with the *substantive reasons given* for making a change. From this vantage point, the crucial issue dividing postliberals and their critics is not *whether* the Christian community is open to critique and change, but how both should be conceptualized. Consider a basketball analogy. Several years ago college basketball instituted a three-point line. The *impetus* for making this change was the desire to make the game more exciting, especially for television audiences; but if this had been the *only* reason that could have been offered, then many would have viewed this as altering the game from the outside. But this basketball change could be and was discussed on basketball's terms (rather than on the terms of television ratings alone). For example, in the past, the rules have favored the tallest players, and so the game came to be dominated by their play. In contrast, the three-point line was supposed to give a greater role to those who were a mere six feet tall. In other words, what was being initiated was not a new game, but a new style of playing the same game. This change attempted to bring about something new while respecting the integrity of the game. Changes within the church take place in a similar manner: the impetus for change may come from any quarter, but change with integrity must be capable of being justified on terms "internal" to the church.[40]

My point is this: critics of postliberalism imply that there are contradictory and competing cultural voices to which the church must listen and by which it must be corrected. If these voices demand that significant aspects of the Christian tradition be left behind, and that new, never-before recognized elements be added, this would seem to pose a potential threat to the integrity of Christianity. Yet the critics of postliberalism seem unconcerned about such prospects. Instead, they assume that certain discourses (which they identify as separate from the Christian faith) should always be given the upper hand — and that Christian claims should be subordinated to them. Gustafson gives the following example of what he has in mind:

> Several years ago I was asked to meet with a denominational group that was writing a statement on "Death and Dying." The first part of the statement was on "Biblical background and basis." I noted that the section ignored a Biblical view that death was caused by the sin of Adam and Eve. I was told that it was not clear from the Bible whether that death was physical, or whether it was spiritual. I cited historic theologians, including Luther, who thought it *was* physical. Then I was told that the whole notion would have to be demythologized in the light of modern knowledge. I suggested that this group had two alternatives: either to say honestly that it no longer believed the tradition or try to demythologize the tradition so the laity could understand why they engage in such work. My point is this: In modern culture few persons with average education any longer *believe* that biological death

is caused by the sins of Adam and Eve, including few who write theology or participate in the Church. A persuasive alternative way of explaining why we die exists. Neither theologians nor people in the churches can avoid it. The tradition, on this point, simply has to be revised because Christian theology and Christian churches are informed by the culture of which they are parts (1985:90–91).

Gustafson fails to offer a third option: the group could have discussed whether it thought the tradition's view of death was central enough to the grammar of the Christian faith to warrant insisting that Christians attempt to recover that insight, despite the apparent difficulty of so doing and despite what they might think about the status of persuasive alternatives. To ignore such an option is to deny the possibility that a perspective from another time or place could radically challenge our contemporary assumptions. The suspicion that these challenges run in only one direction — with the past always being corrected by the present — is confirmed by Gustafson in another context: "Theologians and ethicians have shown remarkable myopia in not taking into account the inferences that can be reasonably drawn from some of the *most secure knowledge we have* of the creation of the universe, the evolution of species, and the likely end of the planet as we know it" (1981:1:97; emphasis added). Ironically, the imperative tone of both remarks — that Christian theology *must* be revised to be brought into line with contemporary thinking — suggests that contemporary ways of thinking may be more insulated from critique than their sectarian challengers!

The "death and dying" example helpfully illustrates the kinds of authorities to which many critics believe the church must listen. What the example fails to show, however, is that there are always clear limits to any process of correction. Because Christians across the ages *have* regarded both Scripture and tradition as ambiguous on this issue, determining their views about death with the aid of other "more authoritative" discourses *may not necessarily* undercut central features of the Christian faith. But if we take an example of a doctrine that is widely considered to be more central to the grammar of the Christian faith, we discover more clearly the kind of correction that could not happen. What would it take for the church to be convinced by "external" experts that Christians have been wrong all these years about Jesus Christ? What would it take for the church to begin teaching that Jesus was simply a human being, like every other human being, and nothing more, and that the church should henceforth stop worshiping him? I believe that this cannot be envisioned, because it requires envisioning a community that advocates the dissolution of that very community. In other words, if the Christian church were to begin teaching that Christians should stop worshiping Jesus, this would be tantamount to teaching that the Christian church should cease to exist as the Christian church. Envisioning that requires something on the order of envisioning that the rules of basketball could be changed in such a way that we would have twenty people playing at a time using something resembling a hockey puck, the point of which was to see how many people you could knock unconscious. This might be a fine game, and one that you would want to commend, but few people would feel good about calling it basketball.

Hence change and critique are always possible within any system or community, but clear limits are also in place. This is why Christians need not take seriously the "findings"

of the so-called Jesus Seminar.[41] That many Christians
are currently abandoning identifiably Christian views of
Jesus for those of the seminar only suggests how confused people are about the role of authorities and the limits
of correction. If Christians follow the recommendations
of the seminar and regard Jesus merely as a first-century
sage, then it remains difficult to determine what is left
of the Christian faith. Christian doctrine serves to define the limits — to define what those who call themselves
Christians agree to affirm about their faith and practice in
order to feel relatively confident that they are still speaking
about the Christian faith and not Islam, New Age, or the
contemporary self-help movements.

The church that understands itself as a contrast-society
is fully capable of engaging the world, even if it chooses
to do so on its own terms. Critics of such a model speak
as if these Christians retreat or withdraw to their enclaves,
ignoring to their detriment the external world that would
force them to correct or adjust their views of the world and
God. But as I have suggested, this way of pitting external
against internal is misleading. The "external" world never
forces itself upon us in this way. Those who have stud-
ied the history and philosophy of science know that even
in science the physical world never forces upon us one and
only one interpretation. In fact, what critics insist are independent or alternative ways of viewing the world are not
necessarily "external" to the church's story at all; rather, the
church, on the basis of its own narrative, might consider
these other stories as interesting, enriching, deficient, misleading, or dangerous ways of knowing about and being
in the world. Consider, for example, an economic view of
the world (complete with congruent narratives, convictions,
and practices) that insisted that people were fundamentally

selfish, but that this selfishness could be used to secure the greatest good for the greatest number if people were allowed to pursue unhindered their own economic self-interest. Such a view of the world and human beings would not be "external" to the church's narrative. On the contrary, such a view might be regarded as a primary example of the church's teaching about the twistedness of human beings, as well as the human penchant for justifying our own selfish desires. In other words, these other stories are not so much external as they are located within the overarching narrative that the church tells about God's relationship with the world and God's people. What, after all, could be external to that? This brings us to the second aspect of the charge of insulation — its perceived impulse to imperialism.

The Impulse to Imperialism

A church that views itself as a contrast-society attempts to take its cues from the story of God's dealings with the world and the people of God as narrated in Scripture. In short, such churches attempt to interpret their present situation, as well as all of reality, in terms of the narrative of Scripture. As Lindbeck insists, this way of interpreting reality

> does not make scriptural contents into metaphors for extrascriptural realities, but the other way round. It does not suggest, as is often said in our day, that believers find their stories in the Bible, but rather that they make the story of the Bible their story. The cross is not to be viewed as a figurative representation of suffering nor the messianic kingdom as a symbol for hope in the future; rather, suffering should be cruciform, and hopes for the future messianic.... It is the

text, so to speak, which absorbs the world, rather than the world the text (1984:118).

To many modern ears, such lofty claims sound dangerously "imperialistic." How can the Christian church be open to critique and correction if its narratives are absorbing everything in the world, including its critics?

In trying to answer this important question, we might begin by examining its central presupposition: Christian narratives are more menacing when *they* function as master narratives than when *other* narratives serve this purpose. To my knowledge no one has stated this presupposition quite this bluntly, but it seems to me to inform much of the Western life in general and criticism of so-called sectarians in particular. This assumption underwrites the widely held Western belief that the far-reaching claims of faith communities who interpret all of reality through those narratives ought to be tempered. This moderation is usually achieved by insisting that these claims be subordinated to or embedded within ostensibly less menacing master narratives. For example, if a community of Christians believes that God calls them to respond to all conflict nonviolently, the implications of this conviction for their public life can be deflected by insisting that this is a purely religious view and therefore applies only to the private realm. Here, the far-reaching claims of the Christian narrative have been stripped of much of their power by embedding them within the master narrative of democratic liberalism — a narrative that teaches us to carve up our lives into public and private spheres and locate "religion" wholly inside the latter.[42]

This example suggests that the criticism leveled against sectarians for being imperialistic cannot simply be a function of their willingness to employ a master narrative.

Everyone seems to employ some form of master narrative, some overarching narrative within which other narratives are embedded, even if this is not openly acknowledged. Thus the question seems not to be *whether* people will employ a master narrative to make sense of the world, but *which one* they will use. Even those who suggest that master narratives are dangerous and thus to be avoided are themselves offering a kind of master narrative — a master narrative that attempts to ensure that different and competing narratives remain different and competing narratives. In such a scheme every narrative is considered to be on a par with every other, and hence not really different after all. This narrative may have much to commend it, but its advocates ought to be honest enough to admit that it functions as an organizing master narrative.

Perhaps what opens certain Christians to derision is not that they employ a master narrative to order their lives, but that they openly employ one that often puts them at odds with those who use other master narratives. This brings us back to a point made earlier. The accusation of sectarianism usually means nothing more than that the group so identified deviates from some widely held norm. But unless one has determined ahead of time that this norm is beyond questioning (and wouldn't such a position amount to insulating it from critique?), then singling out such groups for derision by labeling them sectarian seems unwarranted. What we have are not normal groups and deviant groups, but a clash of groups operating out of different fundamental narratives. Critics of the church-as-contrast-society model presuppose that there is some more fundamental and determinative narrative that is external to the Christian community and by which the Christian community's claims are to be tempered. But why should Christians grant certain "external" narratives a privileged position, especially when such narratives are themselves "internal" to a quite different (and potentially contradictory) way of viewing and living in the world? To take a specific example, it is far from clear why the church's narrative must be embedded within some ostensibly more fundamental narrative, such as that of democratic liberalism, rather than vice versa.

One could plausibly argue that one of the defining marks of modernity is that it has encouraged Christians to interpret their convictions and practices on the basis of what are widely considered more determinative frameworks and narratives. For example, Christians in the West are regularly encouraged to believe that their discourse and practice is best understood by recourse to other more fundamental discourses and practices, such as those of the social sciences. But this assumption is increasingly questioned by Christians. For example, Milbank has mounted an impressive critique against the notion that Christian theology must constantly adjust itself to the knowledge offered it by the social sciences. To subordinate the narratives and practices that shape the Christian faith to a different set of narratives and practices thought to offer more secure knowledge amounts to nothing less than a denial of the central claims that Christian theology has always made. Milbank writes:

> A gigantic claim to be able to read, criticize, say what is going on in other human societies, is absolutely integral to the Christian Church, which itself claims to exhibit the exemplary form of human community. For theology to surrender this claim, to allow that other discourses — "the social sciences" — carry out yet more fundamental readings, would therefore amount to a denial of theological truth. The *logic* of

> Christianity involves the claim that the "interruption" of history by Christ and his bride, the Church, is the most fundamental of events, interpreting all other events. And it is *most especially* a social event, able to interpret other social formations, because it compares them with its own new social practice (1990b:338).

This is a bold and (to modern ears) shocking claim. To those who believe that the church's narrative should be embedded and interpreted within some other set of stories, such a claim amounts to heresy. But as Milbank argues, such a claim is central to what it means to be the church. He writes: "Theology purports to give an ultimate narrative, to provide some ultimate depth of description, because the situation of oneself within such a continuing narrative is what it means to belong to the Church, to be a Christian. However, the claim is made by faith, not a reason which seeks foundations" (1990b:249).

The Christian community is a community of faith that purports to offer an ultimate narrative. This does not mean, however, that these claims of the Christian community are to be accepted as true simply because such claims are made. One can always rightly ask: Why should this narrative be the master narrative? No satisfactory answer to this question is forthcoming if we are looking for the sort of answer that foundationalist epistemologies would encourage us to seek. Nevertheless, there might be reasons for thinking one narrative better than another. Lindbeck rightly argues that although it is impossible to decide between major alternative interpretations or traditions on the basis of reason alone, it is possible to subject theological proposals to "rational testing procedures not wholly unlike those which apply to general scientific theories or paradigms (for which, unlike hypotheses, there are no crucial experiments)" (1984:131). This means that the Christian faith, like other faiths, is not susceptible to "decisive disproof." Our selecting one over another has less to do with proving or disproving certain details of a tradition and more to do with the ability of those traditions to offer a comprehensive, intelligible, and persuasive framework. Hence, Lindbeck suggests that the reasonableness of Christianity (like any faith) "is largely a function of its assimilative powers, of its ability to provide an intelligible interpretation *in its own terms* of the varied situations and realities adherents encounter" (ibid.; emphasis added).[43] This is why Milbank has suggested that if one can speak of the superiority of the Christian faith to other ways of construing and living within the world, such superiority will be evident in the ability of the Christian faith to "out-narrate" other traditions; that is, such superiority will reside in the ability of Christians to offer a more comprehensive, coherent, and gripping story than other traditions (1990b:330).[44]

Both postliberal theologians and those who advocate a church-as-contrast-society model believe that many conflicts and disagreements in Western societies are the product of two (or more) competing master narratives. For many in the West, the liberal democratic narrative remains central. This narrative (or any other proposed alternative) entails, among other things, an ordered set of convictions, practices, and institutions that make sense only within a narrative framework. One central theme of that story is that people are individuals before they are anything else. Individuals are the basic political unit, and their identity *as* individuals is more fundamental than whatever secondary attachments they may secure. Another central theme of the liberal democratic story is that human life can be divided into separate spheres that operate according to their own inner logic and principles. So we have such spheres as economics, politics, religion, law, medicine, and education. The only overarching principles that apply across the board to all these areas are the mythic elements of this larger story — that people should be allowed to pursue their own understanding of happiness unimpeded unless that pursuit brings about demonstrable harm to other people and their similar pursuit. Within this liberal democratic epic, "religion" is that compartment of human life that is most private and contentious. Because human beings cannot agree about issues in this arena (or even agree about criteria for judging their disagreements), we are left to choose our religious preferences with as little interference as possible from the nation-state. This supposed neutrality with regard to religion is one of the touchstones of this story. However, by first identifying the Christian faith as a religion and then embedding it within this larger narrative, liberal democracy turns out to be anything but neutral toward the Christian faith or any other "religion." Any community of faith's claim to particularity or uniqueness is immediately transposed into a difference of religious expression. We see this most clearly when people in the West often presume cavalierly that all world religions are merely different expressions of an underlying and shared truth. This suggests that the narrative of democratic liberalism, with its subtheme of pluralism, often absorbs and consumes other discourses and practices by reframing them in ways that are more in keeping with its own story line (cf. Surin 1990).

Contrary to the claims of its apologists, what liberal democratic societies seem least capable of tolerating is real difference; that is, not merely differences about which principles should govern any given compartment, but about the

whole liberal democratic epic. Such differences seem to be
a major source of irritation for those critics of sectarianism: the so-called sectarians refuse to play by the liberal
democratic rules. These Christians believe that all other
narratives are best read through the narrative of God's particular relationship with the world through Israel, Jesus of
Nazareth, and the church. But this violates the spirit of the
liberal democratic epic, which insists that multiple stories
are always better and that no one story should be taken too
seriously. Indeed, those who take any one story too seriously
are considered to be at best narrow and close-minded (and
at worst sectarians and fanatics). The exceptions to this rule
(about not taking any one story too seriously), are those
who take *very* seriously the liberal democratic story — the
story that says that no story should be taken too seriously.
But instead of regarding themselves as sectarians or fanatics
for elevating this epic to the status of master narrative, they
consider themselves open-minded.

On one level, therefore, Christians who understand the
church as a contrast-society — and who by so doing are
routinely labeled sectarians — are doing nothing more deviant, fanatical, or dangerous than any other group that
reads all of reality on the basis of some overarching narrative. Indeed, they may be engaged in a reading of the
world that is *less* harmful than those of other groups. Advocates of the liberal democratic story, for example, not
only read all of society through this narrative, but insist as
well that all groups within that society make this story the
linchpin of their identity. Although Christians who seek
to embody the church as a contrast-society do believe in
commending to others the advantages of living lives with
this Christian narrative at the center, they also understand
that it would be contradictory to force this "re-reading" on

others. Instead, Christians live in the midst of the world as a contrast-society, praying that God will use their small acts of faithfulness as a witness to the truthfulness of this way of life. In this sense, the Christian narrative might not be "totalizing" in the same way that others are. Indeed, some theologians have argued that the Christian master narrative has internal resources that may aid it in resisting those forms of totalizing discourse that are most dangerous (Middleton and Walsh 1995). For example, Yoder reminds us that when the church insists that all of life and history be read through the historical particularity at the heart of the Christian faith, such an insistence does not condemn it to provincialism, for at the heart of the Christian faith we find two important safeguards:

> One is that this particular celebrating community is missionary. It is defined not by race, nor by geographic isolation, but only by the story itself. This is a story that by its very nature must be shared, and which invites into its celebration all who hear it. Second, this particular particularity is safeguarded against destructive narrowness by the content of its ethic: it forbids itself either to impose its identity or desires on others coercively or to withhold it from any as a privilege. The content of the ethic of this community includes at its heart its affirmation of the dignity of the outside and the adversary in such a way that while the dangers of arbitrary narrowness can never be totally banned, they can at least be warded off. The inner presupposition of particularity is election. By that term here I mean not what later individually concerned Protestant theology has made of it, namely the basis for projections about who knows they will get to heaven,

but the original meaning in our narrative, namely that the story God has chosen to have us tell is the story of some people more than others, of Abraham and Jesus (1994:115).

As Yoder admits, and as the history of the church regrettably testifies, these safeguards provide no guarantees. The temptation to "lord over another" one's particular understanding of the truth can never be removed. But if it cannot be removed, Christians might resist it by appealing to those resources God has entrusted to the church. For this to happen, however, the church would need a strong and confident sense of its own identity and mission in the world. It is to this matter that we now turn our attention.

3

Beyond Sectarianism:
Re-Imagining Church and World

The preceding chapters have argued that the contemporary charges of sectarianism are fraught with problems. This frees us to investigate certain promising models of the church, which in the past have been dismissed as sectarian, without these investigations being short-circuited by such charges. In the remainder of this volume, I would like briefly to sketch one way of construing church and world that I believe holds promise for missionary efforts in the West once we move "beyond sectarianism." First, however, I should explain in what sense I believe the following model takes us "beyond" sectarianism.

All Christians should be urged to eschew any form of separatism that dismembers the body of Christ without regard for reconciliation and healing. Christians in the West (and elsewhere) need to agree that such separatism undermines the integrity of the church's witness to the world. Part of the church's story is that all of God's people remain unfaithful. Yet admitting this does not imply that every congregation or parish is equally faithful or unfaithful; instead, it implies that each should remain open to

God's refining work that often comes at the hands of
the "other," whether those "others" be Christians or non-
Christians. Similarly, churches should remain attentive to
the plaintive cries of those reform movements within and
without their own communities, because history is replete
with examples of how God has used them to call the
church back to a more faithful living witness. Any refor-
mulated model of church and world, therefore, should leave
room for protest and reform without sanctioning schism
and self-righteousness.

Reconfiguring Church and World

I intimated at the beginning of this study that the church in
the West needs to rethink its relationship to "the world." I
also have suggested throughout that such rethinking might
encourage us to consider the church as a contrast-society. In
the past, these groups were often labeled "sects," but I hope
my argument to this point has provided sufficient warrant
for restoring the honorific title "church" to such groups. But
an important question remains: If the church is re-imagined
as a contrast-society, to what exactly is it a contrast?

From the early days of the church, one answer holds
sway: the church is called to be a contrast to "the world."
The potential power of this insight, however, can be recovered only if we rethink our notion of "world" as well.
For example, earlier I noted that many scholars describe as
sectarian any group that offers a distinct response to "the
world." Yet sociologists appear to mean something different from what the early Christians seem to have meant
by contrasting church and world. For example, Johnson
conceptualizes "the world" in sociological terms as "the
social environment in which [the church or sect] exists"

(1963:542). Such a concept of "the world" comes remarkably close to Niebuhr's monolithic notion of culture, for both suggest that the church or sect exists in a wider and in some ways more determinative environment that must be accepted or rejected *in toto*. I have argued earlier that such views are deeply problematic. What would be helpful, therefore, would be a less monolithic and more theologically informed concept of "the world."

One possible starting point would be with Scripture itself, which seems to employ the notion of "the world" in more than one way. Often the phrase "the world" is employed to refer to the whole human realm or even the entire created cosmos — what is at other times simply called "creation" (Matt. 24:21; Rom.1:20; Eph.1:4). When this sense of "the world" is being used, the church is clearly understood as a part of the world, as part of the created order.

Yet a quite different notion of "the world" is also operative in the pages of Scripture. The New Testament also identifies "the world" as those human powers and institutions, as well as the spirits that animate them, that align themselves against the purposes of God. These "principalities and powers," when so aligned, lead necessarily to deficient embodiments of human life and community (Wink 1984). These animating spirits achieve material cultural embodiment through the narratives, practices, convictions, and institutions of human societies. It is in this sense that Paul warns against being conformed to "this world" or "this age," notions that he often uses interchangeably (Rom. 12:2; 1 Cor. 1:20; 2:6–8; 3:18–19; 2 Cor. 4:4; Eph. 2:2).[45] Here we see why and in what sense the church is called to be distinguishable from "the world." By confessing to be disciples of Jesus Christ, the church confesses to its desire and willingness to have its life animated by the Spirit of Christ rather than the spirit of "this (passing) age." And as Yoder reminds us, this means that the distinction between church and world does not simply parallel other dualities to which theologians have sometimes (often unhelpfully) appealed:

> The definition of the gathering of Christians is their confessing Jesus Christ as Lord. The definition of the whole of human society is the absence of that confession, whether through conscious negation or simple ignorance, despite the fact that Christ is ("objectively," "cosmically") Lord for them as well. The duality of church and world is not a slice separating the religious from the profane, nor the ecclesiastical from the civil, nor the spiritual from the material. It is the divide on this side of which there are those who confess Jesus as Lord, who in so doing are both secular and profane, both spiritual and physical, both ecclesiastical and civil, both individual and organized, in their relationships to one another and to others. The difference as to whether Christ is confessed as Lord is a difference on the level of real history and personal choices; not a difference of realms or levels or even dimensions (1994:108–09).

Too often the concepts of church and world are visualized in strictly spatial terms, as if they offer a kind of theological geography. Such a view seems partly to inform those who accuse the church of "withdrawing" from the world. Yet as the above remarks remind us, "church" and "world" are in no straightforward way two distinct places, as if one could retreat or withdraw from the world (in either sense). Those who believe that they are called to have their lives animated by the Spirit of Christ and are thereby called to embody a different "politics" — a different way of ordering social life based on the gospel of Jesus Christ — need not also believe that this necessitates their physical withdrawal from regular contact with those who embody other convictions (cf. 1 Cor. 5:9–10). Indeed, as I will argue below, a proper understanding of the church's service and mission to the world *requires* being in contact with the world. What makes the church different from the world is not that it occupies some different spatial location. The church is different from the world because its life is animated by a different Spirit — a difference manifested in its material practices and institutions, as well as in the narratives and convictions that give them shape and intelligibility.

Christians should regard the world not as a separate place, but as a way of life ordered by a set of narratives, practices, and convictions that is at odds with those narratives, practices, and convictions the church is called to embody as a condition of its discipleship to Jesus Christ. If we re-imagine the world in this way, then we might be in a better position to see the crucial role that narratives play in identifying the animating spirit of any age. What distinguishes communities of Christians from the world is that they respond to all of life by embedding the fragmented and competing narratives of the world within the narrative of God's dealings with creation through Israel, Jesus Christ, and the church. That is, all stories, practices, convictions, and institutions are re-imagined from within this particular narrative framework. Granted, there is more than one way of ordering the potentially conflicting stories, convictions, and loyalties that constitute our lives; nevertheless, part of what it means to be a Christian is to "read" all stories, all practices, all convictions with reference to our discipleship to Jesus and our loyalty to his emerging kingdom. Churches are rightly understood as alternative communities to the extent that they offer a way of ordering life — an alternative way of telling and embodying their stories — that locates who they are and what they should do within a framework quite different, for example, from those frameworks routinely offered by Western societies. In the latter, Christian faith is often perceived to be one (not-so-interesting) lifestyle preference that should be kept within its proper bounds. Within a Christian narrative ordering, however, there is a conscious resistance to Christian convictions and practices being compartmentalized, privatized, and therefore trivialized, because this is seen as denying these convictions and practices precisely the status that they are supposed to have within that narrative, where they are *the* ordering and controlling convictions and practices of Christians' lives.

This way of construing the relationship between church and world offers one potentially promising way of understanding and negotiating membership in multiple communities. It suggests that the peculiar identity of a given community is better grasped in narrative terms (as a group of people who share certain convictions and engage in certain practices on the basis of their orientation to a common story) than in spatial categories (as geographically separable and distinct communities). Even when such spatial categories are used only metaphorically — as when Christians are criticized for "withdrawing" from certain cultural activities — the spatial metaphor remains misleading, because it assumes that Christians were previously located within this sphere and only later withdrew. Instead, Christians should be urged to interpret and narrate their lives as part of the ongoing narrative of the God of Jesus Christ's interaction with God's creation. Or perhaps more accurately, Christians should be encouraged to consider how this narrative of the ongoing work of God in Christ helps them re-imagine their participation in activities that usually offer their own narrative frameworks. If Christians participate in professional societies, trade unions, universities, political parties, nuclear families, and neighborhoods, then they will need to be sure that such participation is entered into and evaluated on the basis of their commitment to God in Christ. In short, a Christian's loyalty to these groups is always penultimate, being circumscribed by his or her overarching loyalty to the God revealed in Jesus Christ. It is when these institutions are regarded as autonomous (as they commonly are in the West), thereby demanding that their narratives stand independent of one another, that participation in multiple communities leads to fragmentation. Lacking the ability to understand how these competing narratives and loyalties might be ordered coherently, people in Western societies often find themselves living lives that feel as if they are populated by "multiple selves," a condition one scholar has aptly termed "multiphrenia" (Gergen 1991).

It would be wrong, however, to imply that the only (or primary) benefit of construing church and world in this way is the potential it holds for resisting the fragmentation that is at the core of much contemporary Western life. More important than this is the promise such a view holds for re-imagining the church's service and mission.

The Church's Service/Mission to the World

This is not the place to survey the many different ways that the church through the years has conceived its mission. This important work has already been begun by others (Bosch 1991). However, a relatively recent chapter of that story *is* of concern here, for it continues to inform and distort much contemporary church thinking and acting with regard to mission. During the last century, churches in the West have often driven a wedge between the church's service to the world and its mission to the world. Part of what enabled this wedge to be driven was the very language used to describe the debate: the church must decide whether its primary focus is "social action" or "evangelism." Unfortunately, each concept was conceived so narrowly that each seemed to exclude the other. For example, focusing on social action often amounted to engaging the world on its own terms rather than on gospel terms. Similarly, focusing on evangelism often amounted to proclaiming the gospel apart from any embodiment that would demonstrate the goodness of this news.[46] This dichotomy encouraged some churches to understand their identity primarily in terms of how socially active they were, whereas others believed their distinctiveness resided in the peculiarity of their beliefs apart from their embodiment. In an odd way, both groups unwittingly reinforced the notion that the church's *own* embodied life before the world was ancillary to the real task of the church. One group of churches assumed that the church was called not to embody a distinctive social alternative, but to cooperate in embodying someone else's social agenda. The other group assumed that its distinctive task was to proclaim a message that could be transmitted and understood apart from the church's living witness.[47]

The church's current confusion about its identity and mission is not simply a consequence of this dichotomy between social concern and evangelism. This confusion also stems from other habits of thought and action that are highly problematic. For example, Christians have too often believed that they held a certain privileged place in God's plan of salvation simply by virtue of their being "saved." As a result, God's election came to be understood primarily with reference to salvation but without reference to mission. In ways remarkably parallel to episodes in the history of ancient Israel, the church came to think of itself as *possessing* salvation rather than as God's *sign* of salvation. Israel's temptation — and now too often the church's temptation — was to forget that it did not exist for itself. God's desire has always been to call out a peculiar people who would serve as a sign of God's present but still future kingdom. By being such a sign, God promised to use this peculiar people to gather the nations (Isa. 60:2–3). Yet as the Roman Catholic biblical scholar Lohfink reminds us, this requires that the people of God live among the nations as God's contrast-society, not for the sake of contradiction, but for the sake of mission:

> The idea of church as contrast-society does not mean contradiction of the rest of society *for the sake of contradiction.* Still less does church as contrast-society mean despising the rest of society due to elitist thought. The only thing meant is contrast *on behalf of others* and *for the sake of others,* the contrast function which is insurpassably expressed in the images "salt of the earth," "light of the world," and "city on a hill" (Matt. 5:13–14). *Precisely because the church does not exist for itself, but completely and exclusively for the world, it is necessary that the church not become the world, that it retain its own countenance.* If the church loses its own contours, if it lets its light be extinguished and its salt become tasteless, then it can no longer transform the

rest of society. Neither missionary activity nor social engagement, no matter how strenuous, helps anymore (1984:146; original emphasis).

Many contemporary churches have forgotten their calling. Many churches no longer strive to be a people whose peculiar character *as* a people might serve as a light to the nations. Yet if these alternative communities we call churches are animated by the Spirit of God rather than "the spirit of the world" (1 Cor. 2:12; cf. 2:6–8), then they will indeed reflect at times, even if imperfectly, the character of God. Such a presence in the midst of the world is both service *and* mission. The church serves the world when it offers the world an alternative way of life — a way of life that God desires for all people. Thus the new humanity that God brings into being through Christ is not so much a *result* of the gospel, as if it could be separated from it, but is itself a crucial *dimension* of that "good news." As René Padilla writes:

Those who have been baptized "into one body" (1 Cor. 12:13) are members of a community in which the differences that separate people in the world have become obsolete. It may be true that "men like to become Christians without crossing racial, linguistic or class barriers," but that is irrelevant. Membership in the body of Christ is not a question of likes or dislikes, but a question of incorporation into a new humanity under the lordship of Christ. Whether a person likes it or not, the same act that reconciles one to God *simultaneously* introduces the person into a community where people find their identity in Jesus rather than in their race, culture, social class or sex, and are consequently reconciled to one another (1983:287).[48]

The church is called into being by the Spirit of Christ in order that its life together may serve as a sign, as a foretaste, and as a herald of the new age inaugurated by Jesus Christ. When the church's embodied life points to this kingdom, offers a foretaste of it, and announces its impending arrival in greater fullness, it does so in the midst of, and in witness to, the old age that "is passing away." Thus the church is called to live in such a way that the world sees, even if only in a fragmentary way, what God's intentions are for the entire created order, which is that the kingdom of the world become the kingdom of our Lord (Rev. 11:15).

One could plausibly argue that much of the church's present feebleness in the West — its inability to offer a persuasive witness to the world — stems from the church's failure to grasp what the world has always known: the embodied life of the church is its most eloquent testimony to the truth and power of the gospel. Unfortunately, this testimony has too often only eloquently validated what skeptics have long believed — that the church is little different from any other community in contemporary life, animated as it is by the spirit of this present age. For example, sociologists have long asserted that the composition of a congregation can be accounted for in strictly sociological terms. The following observation made thirty years ago by Bryan Wilson, which still holds true for many congregations (and not just so-called sectarian ones), stands as a clear indictment of the church's seeming inability to embody an alternative way of life:

> Those who voluntarily associate with each other in a sectarian movement generally show considerable

similarity of social characteristics. Since men of diverse social circumstances do not readily and vol-
untarily associate in any other types of social organization (except where they are "coercively" drawn
together, or stand in distinct and specified status relations and authority relations) it would be surprising to
find them doing so in voluntary religious movements
(1966:184).[49]

How sad that the church offers the world so few surprises.
How sad that churches, which are called to be embodiments of a gospel that breaks down the dividing walls of
hostility, are so often instrumental in rebuilding and sustaining those walls. Indeed, the relative homogeneity that
is a standard feature of most congregations is a scandal
to the gospel, for this homogeneity embodies the (seldom
acknowledged) conviction that our identities are more de-
terminatively shaped and sustained by race, social class,
and level of education than they are by the Spirit of Jesus
Christ.

Such failures are no small matter, for they deeply af-
fect the church's mission to the world. As Hauerwas and
Willimon rightly argue, "the only way for the world to
know that it needs redeeming, that it is broken and fallen,
is for the church to enable the world to strike hard against
something which is an alternative to what the world offers"
(1989:94). The church has not been called out for its own
sake, but for service and witness. As the call of Abraham
reminds us (Gen. 12:1–4), God's plan has always been to
call out a people *through* whom God would bless all people.
Understanding clearly the church's calling is pivotal to any
discernments that the church makes about its responsibili-
ties in and to the world. For example, because the church's

witness to the world cannot be separated from its own life as a sign, foretaste, and herald of the kingdom, the church can ill afford to ignore the character of its life together. This may well mean that the church's "most credible form of witness (and the most 'effective' thing it can do for the world) is the actual creation of a living, breathing, visible community of faith" (:47). Or as Lohfink insists, *the most important and most irreplaceable service Christians can render society is quite simply that they truly be church*" (1984:168; original emphasis).

Suggesting that the churches in the West need to refocus some of their energies "inward" — in order to have something to offer the world — sounds dangerously sectarian to many ears. As was noted earlier, such a position is widely regarded as irresponsible for the way it might encourage a less than robust participation in some (other) "political" activities of society. Yet once we have recognized the relatively narrow view of politics that holds sway in Western societies, then we see that the church — by focusing a measure of its energy on its own embodied life — is not necessarily being politically irresponsible. Rather, it is being politically responsible in a different way — by offering to the world a different political option, a different way of ordering social life. This is why "the church's responsibility to and for the world is first and always to be the church" (Yoder 1994:61). Or as Hauerwas insists:

> Calling for the church to be the church is not a formula for a withdrawal ethic; nor is it a self-righteous attempt to flee from the world's problems; rather it is a call for the church to be a community which tries to develop the resources to stand within the world witnessing to the peaceable kingdom and thus rightly

understanding the world. The gospel is a political gospel. Christians are engaged in politics, but it is a politics of the kingdom that reveals the insufficiency of all politics based on coercion and falsehood and finds the true source of power in servanthood rather than dominion (1983:102).[50]

We noted earlier that many people believe such an alternative politics to be inherently and dangerously totalitarian, based as it is on the practice of embedding all other narratives within the overarching narrative of "God with us." Indeed, for those people who equate sectarianism with fanaticism — with total and uncompromising allegiance — this all-encompassing character of the church as contrast-society is what most offends. These critics would resonate deeply with Wilson's description of sects:

Sects everywhere are allegiance-compelling organizations, seeking to embrace a wide area of the individual's time, thinking, and resources. They demand a monopoly of time, energy, and the terms in which he comprehends the world. They are thus ideologically, and sometimes socially, totalitarian. They confer meaning on events; provide goals; prescribe values; demand particular acts and particular abstentions; they institute authority; they establish new statutes; and — most typically religious function of all — they sanctify and vindicate themselves, their members, their organization, activities, and ideology in incontrovertible terms — terms which a member cannot challenge without becoming an apostate and an enemy (1963b:43).

Wilson's description makes such groups seem so ab-
normal, so extremist, that many people find themselves
reaching immediately for labels such as totalitarian to identify them. Yet we might pause to ask ourselves about the
source of our fear when it comes to the so-called "totalitarian" posture of these communities. What seems to bother
us about these communities is *not* their all-encompassing
vision. After all, there are many other all-encompassing
visions operative in contemporary Western societies that
rarely raise an eyebrow. (To see this, one need only read
back through Wilson's paragraph above, substituting for
the word "sects" the words "economic systems" or "nation-
states.") The objection to such communities, therefore,
must be grounded in the widespread assumption that "religious" groups are somehow more dangerous when they
embody an all-encompassing vision than other entities are
when they do so. Hence, it seems that as long as we accept the category of "religion," which already assumes in its
very grammar a kind of compartmentalization, any attempt
by Christians to embody an all-encompassing vision of life
will be considered aberrant.[51]

This desire to bring everything within the orbit of the
Spirit of Christ does not imply that the church will reject
everything that is *in* the world (understood as creation).
The church will, however, often find it necessary to resist those things that are *of* the world (that is, animated
by a spirit contrary to the Spirit of Christ). Yoder point-
edly sums up the theological basis for "reading" the world
through the church's confession of Jesus' lordship and for
the subsequent process of discernment:

> The church precedes the world epistemologically. We
> know more fully from Jesus Christ and in the context

of the confessed faith than we know in other ways. The meaning and validity and limits of concepts like "nature" or of "science" are best seen not when looked at alone but in the light of the confession of the lordship of Christ. The church precedes the world as well axiologically, in that the lordship of Christ is the center which must guide critical value choices, so that we may be called to subordinate or even to reject those values which contradict Jesus.

Yet both in the order of knowing and in the order of valuing, the priority of the faith does not exclude or deny everything else. Insights which are not contradictory to the truth of the Word incarnate are not denied but affirmed and subsumed within the confession of Christ. Values which are not counter to his suffering servanthood are not rejected but are affirmed and subsumed in his lordship, becoming complementary and instrumental in the exercise of ministry to which he calls his disciples (1984:11).

This underscores one of the fundamental functions of all Christian communities: they serve as communities of discernment. The identity of a Christian community is constituted and sustained by engaging in particular practices that it discerns are appropriate embodiments of its deeply held convictions. Moreover, these practices and convictions are judged sensible to this community because they, along with the "world" in whose midst they are embodied, are located within the ongoing narrative of God's relationship with Israel, Jesus Christ, and the church on behalf of the world. If this is so, then it suggests that the discernment process will be different for Christians than for other people. The operative practices, convictions, and narratives of Christians will often lead them to see different things than the world sees, to name things differently than the world names them, and to respond differently than the world responds. Moreover, Christian communities affirm that this discernment process is enabled and directed by the Spirit of Christ, who was promised to be at work in and through them "where two or three are gathered in my name" (Matt. 18:20).

Christians believe that these differences make it possible for God to use them as a sign, a foretaste, and a herald of the coming kingdom. Further, Christians should not regard their calling to see all of life in relationship to this kingdom as a mere "lifestyle preference." This calling is not simply one among many because this kingdom is not simply one among many. The church believes that God desires to manifest this kingdom — whose character is only imperfectly embodied in the current church — *throughout* the created cosmos. If this were *all* the church believed, it might be tempted (and the church has certainly yielded more than once in its history to this temptation) to try to force the world to be what God will some day make it. But the church must resist this temptation for two reasons, both of which arise out of its own narrative. First, God has given "the world" the freedom to be "the world"; it seems advisable that the church do no less. Even though the church believes that it is called to live in a way that reflects and witnesses to the coming kingdom, it should have no desire to coerce the world to live in this way. To attempt to force the world to stop being the world would not only run counter to the character of the God we serve, but would also amount to asking the world to adopt a way of life for which it has no good reasons. The world (by being the world) lacks the requisite convictions and narratives that would make such a way of life intelligible. This means that although the church must be willing to live its distinct life before the world, it need not be concerned to find a way of forcing the rest of the world to act in this manner.

> This distinctness of the church from the rest of society means that Christians will be making their moral decisions on grounds which not all men and women will apply. The appeal to Christ which gives form to their decisions must then not be measured by whether all will follow it, or by projecting what would happen if they did. Suffering love can be seen as the way to which Christians are called, without our expecting the rest of society all to share in a radical obedience for which it is not prepared (Yoder 1996:75).

Living in the midst of the world as an alternative community requires the ability to function as a community of discernment. Much of this ongoing discernment will be focused on whether the community is being faithful to its call to be an embodied witness *in* and *for* the world without being *of* the world. Without the courage to ask difficult questions about its own life and encourage reform in light of that questioning, the church always risks becoming indistinguishable from the world. As Bloch-Hoell asserts, "the real reason for religious protest is often that the church has changed and has become a mirror of society instead of the salt of the earth" (1978:24–25).

As should be clear by now, this process of discernment does not entail withdrawal. Quite the contrary. Discernment is necessary precisely *because* withdrawal is not an option. In other words, the church is called to engage in the messy process of discernment because the church is not at liberty to make an all or nothing judgment on all cultural expression (whatever that would mean). Only by engaging in Spirit-directed discernment may Christians determine the kind of cultural embodiment called for in any given time and place. In short, faithful discipleship always requires discernment.

Although discipleship demands skill in discernment, this does not guarantee that the church will be so equipped. As indicated earlier, too often the discernment process is undermined by suggestions that the church's only options are to be for or against some monolithic entity called "culture" or "society." For example, Leander Keck rightly observes that most mainline churches have no desire to be countercultural:

> While some voices within the mainline churches call for a countercultural stance in the name of true discipleship, it is altogether unlikely that these churches will heed them. Their whole history makes them tone deaf to such a summons. Besides, most people prefer to be for something and not primarily against the society in which they live, and they prefer making a contribution to it instead of trying to subvert it. In a word, a countercultural stance is for the mainliners not a real option (1993:75–76).

Keck lets the mainliners off the hook too easily. First he leaves unchallenged the locus of their primary allegiance, which he readily admits is not the church but "the society in which they live." Second, Keck dispenses with any need for discernment, for he sanctions the mainliners' resolve to determine beforehand that they will be "for" this "society" rather than "against" it. Finally, he assumes that "contributing" to a society and "subverting" it are opposed to each other. It seems conceivable that churches could contribute robustly to a society by subverting certain features of it.

This leads us to our final consideration. If more churches in the West began to live as contrast-societies, would this make any difference? There is, of course, no way of predicting the kind of impact such communities might have on "the world." More to the point, Christians need not engage in predicting or guaranteeing results. When Jesus sent out the seventy, he did not promise them that they would always be welcomed. Yet if they would do what Jesus was instructing them to do, even when they were received poorly, then they would have the assurance that "the kingdom of God has come near" (Luke 10:11). In the same way, the church's task is not to attempt to ensure that people accept the kingdom. The church's task is to be used by God to bring the kingdom near.[52]

This being said, some may still ask whether there are any reasons to believe that God will indeed use such communities. Ironically, it would appear *narrow-minded* to assume ahead of time that so-called sectarian movements are incapable of impacting those around them, both within and without the church. What is often forgotten is that Troeltsch and Weber, as well as many subsequent scholars in sociology of religion, have been interested in sectarian groups *precisely because* of the "exceptional political and social influence the sectarian forms of Christianity have had in the Western society" (Rasmusson 1995:236). Nevertheless, Lindbeck cautions that in Western societies largely bereft of genuine community, people would likely find enormously appealing such alternative societies as the churches might offer. This experience of community, however, must not be allowed to become its own end, but must be understood (when and if it comes) as the fruit of the church's faithfulness:

> To the extent that the Church becomes a purified yet ecumenical minority, composed of personally committed, not conventional Christians, purged of its present denominational, class, racial and national barriers, it would be able to supply an experience of community which many would treasure above all price. The practical importance of such a transcultural fellowship in helping make mankind more than an amorphous mass might be immense, even though Christians, having their fundamental unity in Christ, would consider this a by-product, a matter of fruit-bearing, rather than the primary purpose of their brotherhood (Lindbeck 1971:239).

Conclusion: Moving Beyond the Labels

The challenges facing the churches, particularly those in the West, are indeed daunting. In societies where the nation-state can no longer be expected to underwrite the church's convictions, the church faces the challenge of re-imagining its mission in and to the world. Part of that revisioning concerns the church's own self-understanding, out of which its service and mission arise. Considerable conversation needs to take place among church people about the kinds of models of church life that are capable of sustaining a faithful identity within and witness to the world. My hope is that this volume makes a small contribution to the vitally-important conversation about the future of the church in contemporary Western societies. This conversation must be allowed to proceed without the charge of sectarianism being hurled at anyone who recommends that the church, in this time and place, understand itself as an alternative community. There are, no doubt, drawbacks to envisioning the church in this or any other way. These need to be discussed seriously and candidly. But such a discussion remains all but impossible as long as people assume that labeling a position as sectarian automatically disqualifies it from serious consideration. There is no way to stop powerful institutions such as the media, the courts, and the educational establishment from using the term "sectarian" in resoundingly pejorative terms. This is not where the real problem lies, however, because Christians can certainly go about the task of seeking to live faithfully, knowing full well that they will often be misunderstood if not scorned. The real problem comes when Christians continue to mimic this name-calling, thereby undercutting fruitful dialogue about how the church might go about discerning the spirits of the age. Yet it need not be this way. If we put away the epithets — sectarian, imperialist, totalitarian — and commit ourselves to such spiritual discernment, by God's grace we may be used to reinvigorate the church's mission and service at the commencement of a new millennium.

Notes

Chapter 1. Different Contexts of Sectarianism

1. On the important role that narratives, practices, and convictions play in forming identity, see Hauerwas and Jones (1989), MacIntyre (1984), and McClendon and Smith (1975).

2. Weber discusses the distinction between "church" and "sect" in several of his works (1946b, 1949:93ff and 1958:144–54). The difference between them stems from what he identifies in another context as the difference between an "ethic of ultimate ends" and an "ethic of responsibility" (1946a:120ff).

3. It should be noted that Troeltsch believed that much of the Protestant church, and not just the Roman Catholic church, fit this type.

4. We should note that Troeltsch's way of putting the matter is deeply problematic, rooted as it is in the distinction between the "religious" and "social" concerns of early Christianity (1960:1:39–43). This distinction makes it possible for him to locate the central concerns of Christianity in the "religious" realm and to see "social" matters as mere expressions of the "religious" ones. In contrast, MacIntyre insists that "a moral philosophy ... characteristically *presupposes* a sociology," and that we have never "fully understood the claims of any moral philosophy until we have spelled out what its social embodiment would be" (1984:23; emphasis added). The same can and ought to be said about theology. As I suggest in the final chapter, every construal of "church" and "world" already presupposes a certain social embodiment. In other words, it is never simply a matter of getting one's view of the church straight and then looking to see what the implications are for something called "social ethics."

5. For example, Dean D. Knudsen, John R. Earle, and Donald W. Shriver, Jr. (1978) have catalogued fourteen different classification schemes that offer anywhere from one to thirteen defining sectarian traits. Two of the most widely cited approaches to this contentious issue are those of Benton Johnson (1963) and Bryan R. Wilson (1963a). When lists of sectarian traits were proliferating at geometric rates, Johnson boldly suggested that churches and sects be distinguished on the basis of a single trait — the relationship of the group to the surrounding social environment. He writes: "A church is a religious group that accepts the social environment in which it exists. A sect is a religious group that rejects the social environment in which it exists" (:542). Wilson, on the other hand, proposed a complex and highly nuanced typology of seven different kinds of sects. Although the details of this complex typology are beyond the scope of this study, it is striking that Wilson also acknowledges that his typology "takes as its central criterion the sect's *response to the world*" (:363). Though neither Johnson nor Wilson has any overtly theological concerns, it is instructive that their very different projects agree on this central point: that whatever a sect is in a sociological sense, it has as its defining feature a distinct response to the world. This observation will be taken up theologically in chapter 3.

6. Duane K. Friesen (1975) has exposed some of the normative features of Troeltsch's typology, while its limited applicability has been noted by many scholars, including Johnson (1963).

7. Not surprisingly, Niebuhr has himself been subsequently criticized for all but assuming the utter necessity of this transformation. See, for example, Bryan R. Wilson (1959 and 1990:105–27).

8. As several subsequent scholars have noted, Niebuhr seems to be pointing to the Old Order Amish here, not the Mennonites. See Yoder (1996:34).

9. As Jaroslav Pelikan writes: "In its earliest Christian use, the term 'heresy' was not sharply distinguished from 'schism'; both referred to factiousness" (1971:69). Pelikan goes on to note that Augustine and Basil (among others) came to distinguish between heresy and schism, with heresy involving false doctrine and schism being dissident but orthodox. In practice, the distinction has been difficult to maintain consistently, not least because schismatics, when

and if they separated themselves from the rest of the body, were considered to have a heretical view of the church. This is why the Novatianists were considered by many to be heretics as well as schismatics, even though they were in most respects quite orthodox. As is well known, the difficulty of resolving disagreements about such matters was compounded because there was no agreed-upon way to determine which side in a dispute represented the "true" church. See also S. L. Greenslade (1953).

10. The English term "sectarian" itself (or "sectary") was apparently first used in the seventeenth and eighteenth centuries by the Presbyterians with reference to the Independents, subsequently by the Roman Catholics with reference to any of the Protestants, and especially by the Anglicans with reference to the Protestant Nonconformists. See *The Compact Edition of the Oxford English Dictionary* (Oxford University Press, 1971), II:2703. Such usage remains today when sects are considered primarily as "spin-offs" from more established churches or religions. See, for example, Finke and Stark (1992).

11. With reference to the Donatists, Augustine writes: "The clouds roll with thunder, that the House of the Lord shall be built throughout the earth: and these frogs sit in their marsh and croak— We are the only Christians." Quoted in Peter Brown (1967:221).

12. For a historical overview of the Boston movement, see Hughes (1996:357–63). Throughout his work Hughes makes considerable use of the sociological distinctions between church, sect, and denomination, arguing that on the American scene groups of Christians must choose whether to be a denomination or a sect, for disestablishment rules out the possibility of their being a church in the Troeltschian sense.

13. The literature on the foundationalist, antifoundationalist, and nonfoundationalist debate is voluminous and cuts across traditional disciplinary lines. See, for example, Rorty (1979), Bernstein (1985), Mitchell (1985), Herzog (1985), Hauerwas, Murphy, and Nation (1994), Thiel (1994), and Phillips (1995).

14. In philosophical circles, Alasdair MacIntyre remains one of the most articulate advocates of epistemological sectarianism (1984 and 1988). Although there is no agreed-upon list of postliberal theologians, the movement is often associated with the works of

Yale theologians George Lindbeck (1984) and Hans Frei (1974 and 1986). Their work is an explicit attempt to move beyond the liberal conception of "religion" dominant in the West, where religion is conceived primarily in terms of "experience" and the expression of that experience. Those unfamiliar with these debates should be cautioned that the word "liberal" in this context has nothing to do with the epithet politicians (particularly in the United States) regularly hurl at each other.

15. Anson Phelps Stokes writes: "It was the enormous Irish immigration of the middle of the century, with the growing urbanization that accompanied it, that contributed more than any other factor to the determination to develop a public school system which, while entirely undenominational, should conserve all that was considered best in the American educational tradition as developed mainly under New England leadership. It was essentially a democratic and constructive movement, for there were large elements in the population that showed a definite fear that the new immigrants, whose usefulness to the country was somewhat reluctantly granted, might, without a new emphasis on public education unconnected with any Church, introduce unwelcome changes in the American creed." Stokes notes that there were only 800 public high schools in the United States in 1880; by 1944 there were 28,973 (1950:2:67, 488).

16. For example, by 1918 the Supreme Court of Iowa acknowledged this widespread consensus: "If there is any one thing which is well settled in the policies and purposes of the American people as a whole, it is the fixed and unalterable determination that there shall be an absolute and unequivocal separation of church and state, and that our public school system, supported by the taxation of the property of all alike — Catholic, Protestant, Jew, Gentile, believer and infidel — shall not be used directly or indirectly for religious instruction, and above all that it shall not be made an instrument of proselyting influence in favor of any religious organization, sect, creed or belief." *Knowlton* v. *Baumhover* (1918), as quoted in Stokes (1950:2:69).

17. For example, Stephen Carter (1993) writes: "Protestants, interestingly, relied on the public schools, perhaps out of a faith that

those schools already reflected their dominant values. This last point bears emphasis. Many Catholics and Jews fled the public schools for just that reason — that a dominant *sectarian* ethos was, in their judgment, being taught to their kids" (:203; original emphasis).

18. This is how Lawrence A. Cremin (1988) describes the habits of thought of Josiah Strong and other evangelical educational visionaries at the end of the nineteenth century (:115).

19. It is interesting to note that the term *fanatic* has for some time been used in alliance with the term *sectarian,* as for example, during the last half of the seventeenth century to apply to the Nonconformists. The following comment was made by the Anglican historian Thomas Fuller in his *Mixt Contemplations in Better Times,* published in 1660: "A new word coined, within few months, called fanatics, seemeth well proportioned to signify the sectaries of our age." See *OED,* I:959.

20. Kelley Shannon, Associated Press Writer, "Agent Testifies He Saw Branch Davidian Lighting Fire At End of Standoff," February 7, 1994; emphasis added. An AP story by the same writer that ran a few weeks earlier (January 12) had noted that the defense lawyers had asked the court to bar prosecutors from using the words "cult" and "compound," because the terms were so obviously prejudicial. The judge apparently did not understand the potential harm: he ruled that the prosecutors could use the terms, because "that property has been referred to as a compound one zillion times by the members of the media."

21. Associated Press, "ATF Agent Sues Over Failed Davidian Raid," June 11, 1994; emphasis added.

22. Arieh O'Sullivan, Associated Press Writer, "Standoff Ends as Armed Cult Members Surrender," May 11, 1994.

Chapter 2. The Presuppositions Behind the Contemporary Charge

23. The contemporary epistemological debates in the philosophy of science suggest that nonfoundational approaches are making headway in all disciplines. For a relatively modest proposal, see the suggestive article by John Hardwig (1991).

24. For those unfamiliar with the phrases "liberal democracy" or "democratic liberalism," the words "liberal" or "liberalism" are not epithets but point to certain tenets of and practices fostered by a political philosophy common in Western societies. Ronald Beiner writes: "The starting point for an understanding of liberalism is the notion that there is a distinctive liberal way of life, characterized by the aspiration to increase and enhance the prerogatives of the individual by maximal mobility in all directions, throughout every dimension of social life (in and out of particular communities, in and out of socioeconomic classes, and so on); and by a tendency to turn all areas of human activity into matters of consumer preference; a way of life based on progress, growth, and technological dynamism.... This liberal mode of existence is marked by tendencies toward pluralistic fragmentation, but paradoxically it is also marked by tendencies toward universalism and even homogenization.... Liberalism, no less than socialism, feudalism, or any other social order, is a global dispensation — that is, a way of life that excludes other ways of life. It does no good for the liberal to say that the liberal state is neutral between the diverse life-choices of individuals. Is it neutral about continual growth and higher productivity? Is it neutral about scientific progress? Is it neutral about the market as a means of maximizing consumer choices? The fact that all of this supposedly enhances the prerogatives of individuals in the design of their life-options is what actually defines this dispensation rather than showing that there is none" (1992:22–23, 24).

25. Another possible mode of "engagement" has been suggested by John Howard Yoder. He suggests that we would do well to retain a distinction between the language we might use to appeal to the conscience of our rulers (which will normally be their own language) and the language of our discipleship. He writes: "If the ruler claims to be my benefactor, and he always does, then that claim provides me as his subject with the language I can use to call him to be more humane in his ways of governing me and my neighbors. The language of his moral claims is not the language of my discipleship, nor are the standards of his decency usually to be identified with those of my servanthood. Yet I am quite free to use his language to reach him" (1984:158).

26. Williams (1983:87–93) argues that the word "culture" is one of the "two or three most complicated words in the English language." Readers interested in tracing these complexities would do well to start with Williams's overview.

27. This quotation is one of the few places in Niebuhr's book where the plural "cultures" is used. However, the context suggests that he is speaking in a global context, which is why he speaks of both "societies" and "cultures." Such plural usage, therefore, is fully consonant with his singular and monolithic view of culture that "lays its claim on every Christian."

28. Compare the recent comment of Leander Keck, with reference to what he calls the "countercultural" church: "Nor should it surprise us if the countercultural church, having demonized non-Christian elements in society, can scarcely avoid living in a Manichaean world, where the Redeemer is not the Creator but the Creator's adversary" (1993:75). Although Keck does not identify whom he has in mind when he speaks of the counterculturalists, it hardly matters. What *is* important is that the notion of being countercultural as a general posture can be linked with Manichaeism only if one views culture as monolithic.

29. It is ironic that Niebuhr prefaces his discussion of these two terms, "Christ" and "culture," with the observation that "we shall need to exercise care lest we prejudge the issue by so defining one term or the other or both that only one of the Christian answers to be described will appear legitimate" (1951:11). Yet this appears to be exactly what Niebuhr has done, for by making culture monolithic he has assured that two of the positions will of necessity be seen as extreme (because they reject or accept "the culture" *in toto*), whereas the "moderating" positions (and especially the transformationist position) will be seen as more adequate.

30. I am indebted to Yoder's recently published essay (1996), which has circulated for many years in typescript, for pointing out the monolithic character of Niebuhr's concept of culture. My discussion in this section closely follows Yoder's account.

31. For an example of the classical view, see Aristotle's *Politics*, which not only insists that human beings are by nature "political

animals," but discusses the importance of social order for human flourishing.

32. Milbank makes a similar point: "Any conception of religion as designating a realm within culture, for example, that of spiritual experience, charismatic power, or ideological legitimation, will tend to reflect merely the construction of religion within Western modernity" (1990a:177).

33. Milbank writes: "Secular reason claims that there is a 'social' vantage point from which it can locate and survey various 'religious' phenomena. But it has turned out that assumptions about the nature of religion themselves help to define the perspective of this social vantage. From a deconstructive angle, therefore, the priority of society over religion can always be inverted, and every secular positivism is revealed to be also a positivist theology. Given this insight, sociology could still continue, but it would have to redefine itself as a 'faith'" (1990b:139).

34. For evidence that the church has not always considered economic matters as peripheral to its identity, see González (1990) and Meeks (1989).

35. In an article aptly entitled "On the Fringe of Christendom," Wilson writes: "The loss of roots, the diminished role of the family and of kinship relations, and the attenuation of man's allegiance to any given locality group, may make even advanced society continually vulnerable to sect expression as a source of security and identity in a world too much in flux" (1963b:50). It might be well to note at this point that many Christians are beginning to acknowledge that being "on the fringe of Christendom" is not such a bad place to be.

36. I have dealt at greater length with this issue in a separately published essay (Kenneson 1996), from which much of what follows is taken.

37. I do not mean to imply either that all postliberal theologians advocate a church-as-contrast-society model, or that those who do advocate such a model are dependent upon postliberal insights for their position. Neither position requires the other for its intelligibility. My impression, however, is that both positions name many of the issues in similar ways. Because postliberal theologians have articulated many of these issues in professional theological circles,

they have often become the specific target of critics. My sense is that most of these criticisms would apply equally to those groups of Christians who see themselves as a distinct community in contrast to the surrounding society.

38. In making this distinction, I am indebted to Bruce D. Marshall's essay (1990b).

39. On the parallels between the prohibitions of Acts 15 and Leviticus 18–19, see Raymond E. Brown and John P. Meier (1983:3).

40. Although there is not room to pursue the point here, I think other examples from the history of the church abound. For example, certain forgotten nonliteral readings of Genesis have been recovered largely as a result of the impetus of contemporary science. Perhaps certain lessons that the church has learned or might learn from the civil rights movement, the women's movement, the environmental movement, and the contemporary emphasis on multiculturalism could be helpfully conceptualized by distinguishing between the impetus for change and the internal reasons given for that change.

41. For a view of Jesus informed by the Jesus Seminar, see Funk (1996); for a critique of the entire enterprise of the seminar, see Johnson (1996).

42. Another example of this domestication process is the way in which the writings of Joseph Campbell (1972) and others are commonly used to locate the particular claims of Christianity within a more determinative framework. In other words, many people have learned that they need not take the claims of Christianity seriously because they believe that Jesus is merely one manifestation of "the hero with a thousand faces." I owe this example to Margaret Adam.

43. In explaining such "assimilative powers," Marshall writes: "The scripturally shaped web of Christian belief will be warranted as the primary criterion of truth by its capacity, evinced in repeated successes, to internalize or assimilate initially alien discourse, that is, to give persuasive interpretations in its own terms of such discourse which allow that discourse to be held true, or which give compelling reasons in light of its own criteria to account for rejecting that discourse as false. Conversely, repeated failure to assimilate alien discourse or to give compelling reasons for rejecting it will ar-

gue that we are not warranted in ascribing justificatory primacy to the plain sense of Scripture" (1990b:78).

44. This is not to suggest that this gives the church some decisive advantage or leverage that could then be used to sponsor triumphalism. Rather, Milbank himself would likely be the first to remind us that there is no neutral standpoint from which to judge who tells the most comprehensive and adequate story; this too is a matter of judgment made from within particular communities.

Chapter 3. Beyond Sectarianisms: Re-Imagining Church and World

45. Occasionally, such varied usage leads to ambiguity, as when Paul asserts that "in Christ God was reconciling the world to himself" (2 Cor. 5:19). Here Paul could mean that in Christ God was reconciling all of sinful and fallen *humanity* to himself, or he could mean (as the letters to the Ephesians and Colossians suggest) that this reconciling work is cosmic in scope. The same could be argued about such classic passages as John 3:16.

46. A clear acknowledgment of this problem was recognized by several hundred delegates at the International Congress on World Evangelization that met at Lausanne in 1974. This group criticized the Lausanne Covenant for perpetuating this false dichotomy. They insisted that "there is no biblical dichotomy between the word spoken and the word made visible in the lives of God's people. Men will look as they listen and what they see must be at one with what they hear.... There are times when our communication may be by attitude and action only, and times when the word spoken will stand alone: but we must repudiate as demonic the attempt to drive a wedge between evangelism and social concern" (quoted in Bosch 1991:406). Although this was a good place to start, I would want to make an even stronger statement. I would argue that any "word spoken" is always already an embodied word. Thus the issue is not whether the church will attach an embodiment to its spoken words, like some appendage, but how the character of its current embodiment reinforces or undermines its spoken message.

47. This is not, of course, to suggest that the church should avoid cooperating with others as it seeks to serve "the world." The church

should, however, attempt to do so as an embodiment of the gospel story rather than as the embodiment of some other story. Similarly, I in no way intend to downplay the significance of Christian convictions. The church must remember, however, that such convictions form only part of the web of the Christian faith (along with its narratives, practices, and institutions).

48. The internal quotation is from McGavran (1970:198). Padilla goes on to argue that this social dimension of the gospel is evident throughout the New Testament and was crucial to the church's mission: "No research is necessary to verify that the congregations that resulted from the Gentile mission normally included Jews and Gentiles, slaves and free, rich and poor, and were taught that in Christ all the differences derived from their respective homogeneous units had become irrelevant (Eph. 6:5–9; Col. 3:33–4:1; 1 Tim. 6:17–19; Philem. 16; James 1:9–11; 2:1–7; 4:13; 1 Pet. 2:18; 1 John 3:17). The impact that the early church made on non-Christians *because of Christian brotherhood across natural barriers* can hardly be overestimated. In F. F. Bruce's words, 'Perhaps this was the way in which the gospel made the deepest impression on the pagan world' (Bruce 1957:277)" (:299).

49. This echoes, of course, the earlier judgment that H. Richard Niebuhr had pronounced on the hypocrisy of denominationalism: "[Denominationalism] is a compromise, made far too lightly, between Christianity and the world. Yet it often regards itself as a Christian achievement and glorifies its martyrs as bearers of the Cross. It represents the accommodation of Christianity to the caste-system of human society. . . . The division of the churches closely follows the division of men into the castes of national, racial, and economic groups. It draws the color line in the church of God; it fosters the misunderstandings, the self-exaltations, the hatreds of jingoistic nationalism by continuing in the body of Christ the spurious differences of provincial loyalties; it seats the rich and poor apart at the table of the Lord, where the fortunate may enjoy the bounty they have provided while others feed upon the crusts their poverty affords" (1929:6).

50. A powerful summary of this view of the relationship between church and world appears in an appendix to Garrett (1969:318):

"The congregation is called out of the wider society for a communal existence within and for, yet distinct from, the structures and values of the rest of the world. This distinctness from the world is the presupposition of a missionary and servant ministry to the world. At times it demands costly opposition to the powers of the world. We reject any view of the world which fails to reckon with its fallenness and any view of the church which simply identifies her membership, or her goals, with the world in its rebelliousness. We are left with the danger of misunderstanding separation from the world in terms of geographic or social distance or of a merely ethical or cultural nonconformity, and with the further danger of precipitately applying the concept of separation from the world to other Christians from whom we differ."

51. In a book that was published as I was completing this manuscript, Rodney Clapp argues that "the real alternatives, if we want to use nasty-sounding names, are between sectarianism and syncretism. That is, we are all marked by time, place and limited communities. The sectarian is one who strives to be marked by one predominant community. The syncretist, like the ancient Greek mystery religion adherents who invoked one god for fertility and another for success in business, is happy to belong to and serve a number of communities of more or less equal authority. The sectarian accordingly desires a more holistic, unified life, the syncretist a compartmentalized, unabashedly eclectic life. But neither, let it once more be noted, escapes history and limited perspective" (1996:145–46).

52. I am indebted to my colleague J. Lee Magness for this insight into Luke's account.

References Cited

Asad, Talal. 1993. *Genealogies of Religion: Discipline and Reasons of Power in Christianity and Islam.* Baltimore: Johns Hopkins University Press.

Beiner, Ronald. 1992. *What's the Matter with Liberalism?* Berkeley: University of California Press.

Bernstein, Richard J. 1985. *Beyond Objectivism and Relativism: Science, Hermeneutics, and Praxis.* Philadelphia: University of Pennsylvania Press.

Bloch-Hoell, Nils E. 1978. The Church and Religious Protest. In *The Church in a Changing Society.* Pp. 21–27.

Bosch, David J. 1991. *Transforming Mission: Paradigm Shifts in Theology of Mission.* Maryknoll, N.Y.: Orbis Books.

Brown, Peter. 1967. *Augustine of Hippo.* Berkeley: University of California Press.

Brown, Raymond E. and John P. Meier. 1983. *Antioch and Rome: New Testament Cradles of Catholic Christianity.* New York: Paulist Press.

Bruce, F. F. 1957. *Commentary on the Epistle to the Colossians.* London: Marshall, Morgan & Scott.

Brueggemann, Walter. 1985. II Kings 18–19: The Legitimacy of a Sectarian Hermeneutic. *Horizons in Biblical Theology* 7 (June):1–42.

Campbell, Joseph. 1972. *The Hero with a Thousand Faces.* 2d ed. Princeton: Princeton University Press.

Carter, Stephen. 1993. *The Culture of Disbelief: How American Law and Politics Trivialize Religious Devotion.* New York: Basic Books.

Casanova, José. 1994. *Public Religions in the Modern World.* Chicago: University of Chicago Press.

Cavanaugh, William T. 1995. "A Fire Strong Enough to Consume the House": The Wars of Religion and the Rise of the State. *Modern Theology* 11:4 (October):397–420.

The Church in a Changing Society. 1978. Proceedings of the CIHEC-Conference in Uppsala. Uppsala, Sweden: Almqvist & Wiksell.

Clapp, Rodney. 1996. *A Peculiar People: The Church as Culture in a Post-Christian Society.* Downers Grove, Ill.: InterVarsity Press.

Cremin, Lawrence A. 1988. *American Education: The Metropolitan Experience, 1876–1980.* New York: Harper & Row.

D'Costa, Gavin, ed. 1990. *Christian Uniqueness Reconsidered: The Myth of a Pluralistic Theology of Religions.* Maryknoll, N.Y.: Orbis Books.

Eastland, Terry, ed. 1993. *Religious Liberty in the Supreme Court: The Cases that Define the Debate over Church and State.* Washington, D.C.: Ethics and Public Policy Center.

Finke, Roger, and Rodney Stark. 1992. *The Churching of America, 1776–1990: Winners and Losers in Our Religious Economy.* New Brunswick, N.J.: Rutgers University Press.

Fish, Stanley. 1989. *Doing What Comes Naturally: Change, Rhetoric, and the Practice of Theory in Literary and Legal Studies.* Durham, N.C.: Duke University Press.

Flowers, Ronald B. 1994. *That Godless Court? Supreme Court Decisions on Church-State Relationships.* Louisville: Westminster John Knox Press.

Frei, Hans W. 1974. *The Eclipse of Biblical Narrative: A Study in Eighteenth and Nineteenth Century Hermeneutics.* New Haven: Yale University Press.

———. 1986. The "Literal Reading" of Biblical Narrative in the Christian Tradition: Does It Stretch or Will It Break? In McConnell 1986:36–77.

Friesen, Duane K. 1975. Normative Factors in Troeltsch's Typology of Religious Association. *Journal of Religious Ethics* 3:2 (Fall):271–83.

Funk, Robert W. 1996. *Honest to Jesus: Jesus for a New Millennium.* San Francisco: HarperSanFrancisco.

Garrett, James Leo, Jr., ed. 1969. *The Concept of the Believers' Church.* Scottdale, Pa.: Herald Press.

Gergen, Kenneth. 1991. *The Saturated Self: Dilemmas of Identity in Contemporary Life.* New York: Basic Books.

Gerth, H. H., and C. Wright Mills, eds. 1946. *From Max Weber: Essays in Sociology.* New York: Oxford University Press.

Gilbert, Arthur. 1961. A Catalogue of Church-State Problems. *Religious Education* 56:6 (Nov.-Dec.):424–30.

González, Justo L. 1990. *Faith and Wealth: A History of Early Christian Ideas on the Origin, Significance, and Use of Money.* San Francisco: Harper & Row.

Graham, Stephen R. 1995. *Cosmos in the Chaos: Philip Schaff's Interpretation of Nineteenth Century American Religion.* Grand Rapids: Eerdmans.

Greenslade, S. L. 1953. *Schism in the Early Church.* New York: Harper & Brothers.

Gustafson, James M. 1981. *Ethics from a Theocentric Perspective.* Vol. 1. Chicago: University of Chicago Press.

———. 1985. The Sectarian Temptation: Reflections on Theology, the Church, and the University. *Proceedings of the Catholic Theological Society* 40:83–94.

Hardwig, John. 1991. The Role of Trust in Knowledge. *The Journal of Philosophy* 88:12 (Dec):693–708.

Hauerwas, Stanley. 1983. *The Peaceable Kingdom: A Primer in Christian Ethics.* Notre Dame: University of Notre Dame Press.

Hauerwas, Stanley, and L. Gregory Jones, eds. 1989. *Why Narrative? Readings in Narrative Theology.* Notre Dame: University of Notre Dame Press.

Hauerwas, Stanley, Nancey Murphy, and Mark Nation, eds. 1994. *Theology Without Foundations: Religious Practice and the Future of Theological Truth.* Nashville: Abingdon Press.

Hauerwas, Stanley, and William H. Willimon. 1989. *Resident Aliens.* Nashville: Abingdon Press.

Herzog, Don. 1985. *Without Foundations: Justification in Political Theory.* Ithaca: Cornell University Press.

Hughes, Richard T. 1996. *Reviving the Ancient Faith: The Story of Churches of Christ in America.* Grand Rapids: Eerdmans.

Johnson, Benton. 1963. On Church and Sect. *American Sociological Review* 28 (Aug.):539–49.

Johnson, Timothy Luke. 1996. *The Real Jesus: The Misguided Quest for the Historical Jesus and the Truth of the Traditional Gospels.* San Francisco: HarperSanFrancisco.

Jones, L. Gregory. 1995. *Embodying Forgiveness: A Theological Analysis.* Grand Rapids: Eerdmans.

Kaufman, Peter Iver. 1982. Sectarian Protestantism and Political Culture. In *In the Great Tradition: Essays on Pluralism, Voluntarism, and Revivalism.* Ed. Joseph D. Ban and Paul R. Dekar. Valley Forge: Judson Press. Pp. 75–89.

Keck, Leander. 1993. *The Church Confident.* Nashville: Abingdon Press.

Kelsey, David H. 1990. Church Discourse and Public Realm. In Marshall 1990a 7–34.

Kenneson, Philip D. 1996. The Alleged Incorrigibility of Postliberal Theology. In *The Nature of Confession: Evangelicals and Postliberals in Conversation.* Ed. Timothy R. Phillips and Dennis L. Okholm. Downers Grove, Ill.: InterVarsity Press. Pp. 93–106.

Knudsen, Dean D., John R. Earle, and Donald W. Shriver, Jr. 1978. The Conception of Sectarian Religion: An Effort at Clarification. *Review of Religious Research* 20 (Fall):44–60.

Lindbeck, George A. 1971. The Sectarian Future of the Church. In *The God Experience: Essays in Hope.* Ed. Joseph P. Whelan, S.J. New York: Paulist Press. Pp. 226–43.

———. 1984. *The Nature of Doctrine: Religion and Theology in a Postliberal Age.* Philadelphia: Westminster Press.

Lohfink, Gerhard. 1984. *Jesus and Community: The Social Dimension of Christian Faith.* Philadelphia: Fortress Press.

Lovsky, Fadeiy. 1991. The Churches and the Sects. *One in Christ* 27:3:222–33.

MacIntyre, Alasdair. 1984. *After Virtue.* 2d ed. Notre Dame: University of Notre Dame Press.

———. 1988. *Whose Justice? Which Rationality?* Notre Dame: University of Notre Dame Press.

Marshall, Bruce D., ed. 1990a. *Theology and Dialogue: Essays in Conversation with George Lindbeck*. Notre Dame: University of Notre Dame Press.

———. 1990b. Absorbing the World: Christianity and the Universe of Truths. In Marshall 1990a: 69–102.

Mathisen, Robert R., ed. 1982. *The Role of Religion in American Life: An Interpretive Historical Anthology*. Lanham, Md.: University Press of America.

McClendon, James W., Jr., and James M. Smith. 1975. *Understanding Religious Convictions*. Notre Dame: University of Notre Dame Press.

McConnell, Frank D. 1986. *The Bible and the Narrative Tradition*. New York: Oxford University Press.

McGavran, Donald. 1970. *Understanding Church Growth*. Grand Rapids: Eerdmans.

Meeks, M. Douglas. 1989. *God the Economist: The Doctrine of God and Political Economy*. Minneapolis: Fortress Press.

Middleton, J. Richard, and Brian Walsh. 1995. Facing the Postmodern Scalpel: Can the Christian Faith Withstand Deconstruction? In *Christian Apologetics in the Postmodern World*. Ed. Timothy R. Phillips and Dennis L. Okholm. Downers Grove, Ill.: InterVarsity Press. Pp. 131–54.

Milbank, John. 1990a. The End of Dialogue. In D'Costa 1990:174–91.

———. 1990b. *Theology and Social Theory: Beyond Secular Reason*. Oxford: Basil Blackwell.

Miscamble, Wilson D. 1987. Sectarian Passivism? *Theology Today* 44:1 (April):69–77.

Mitchell, W. J. T., ed. 1985. *Against Theory: Literary Studies and the New Pragmatism*. Chicago: University of Chicago Press.

Neusner, Jacob. 1975. *Christianity, Judaism and Other Greco-Roman Cults*. Part 2. *Early Christianity*. Leiden: E. J. Brill.

Nevin, John Williamson. 1848. The Sect System. In Yrigoyen, Jr., and Bricker 1978:128–73.

Newbigin, Lesslie. 1995. *Proper Confidence: Faith, Doubt and Certainty in Christian Discipleship*. Grand Rapids: Eerdmans.

Niebuhr, H. Richard. 1929. *The Social Sources of Denominationalism*. New York: Henry Holt & Co; Reprint edition. New York: Meridian Books, 1957.

———. 1951. *Christ and Culture*. New York: Harper & Row.

Padilla, C. René. 1983. The Unity of the Church and the Homogeneous Unit Principle. In Wilbert R. Shenk, 1983:285–303.

Pelikan, Jaroslav. 1971. *The Christian Tradition*. Vol. 1: *The Emergence of the Catholic Tradition* (100–600). Chicago: University of Chicago Press.

Pfeffer, Leo. 1975. *God, Caesar, and the Constitution: The Court as Referee of Church-State Confrontation*. Boston: Beacon Press.

Phillips, D. Z. 1995. *Faith After Foundationalism*. Boulder, Colo.: Westview Press.

Quirk, Michael J. 1987. Beyond Sectarianism? *Theology Today* 44:1 (April):78–86.

Rasmusson, Arne. 1995. *The Church as* Polis: *From Political Theology to Theological Politics as Exemplified by Jürgen Moltmann and Stanley Hauerwas*. Notre Dame: University of Notre Dame Press.

Rorty, Richard. 1979. *Philosophy and the Mirror of Nature*. Princeton: Princeton University Press.

Scroggs, Robin. 1975. The Earliest Christian Communities as Sectarian Movement. In Neusner 1975:1–23.

Shenk, Wilbert R., ed. 1983. *Exploring Church Growth*. Grand Rapids: Eerdmans.

Stackhouse, Max L. 1987. Christian Social Ethics as a Vocation. Presidential Address to the Society of Christian Ethics, 1987. *The A.M.E. Zion Quarterly Review* 99:1 (April):9–18.

Stassen, Glen H., D. M. Yeager, and John Howard Yoder. 1996. *Authentic Transformation: A New Vision of Christ and Culture*. Nashville: Abingdon Press.

Stokes, Anson Phelps. 1950. *Church and State in the United States*. 3 Volumes. New York: Harper & Brothers.

Surin, Kenneth. 1990. A "Politics of Speech": Religious Pluralism in the Age of the McDonald's Hamburger. In D'Costa 1990:192–212.

Tegborg, Lennart. 1978. The Disappearance of an American Dream: The New York Prayer Case in 1962 in the Public Debate. In *The Church in a Changing Society*. Pp. 166–71.

Thiel, John E. 1994. *Nonfoundationalism*. Minneapolis: Fortress Press.

Thiemann, Ronald F. 1985. *Revelation and Theology: The Gospel as Narrated Promise*. Notre Dame: University of Notre Dame Press.

———. 1991. *Constructing a Public Theology: The Church in a Pluralistic Culture*. Louisville: Westminster/John Knox Press.

Toulmin, Stephen. 1990. *Cosmopolis: The Hidden Agenda of Modernity*. New York: Free Press.

Troeltsch, Ernst. 1960. *The Social Teaching of the Christian Churches*. 2 Volumes. New York: Harper & Brothers. German original 1911.

Weber, Max. 1946a. Politics as a Vocation. In Gerth and Mills 1946:77–128. German original 1919.

———. 1946b. The Protestant Sects and the Spirit of Capitalism. In Gerth and Mills 1946:302–22.

———. 1949. *The Methodology of the Social Sciences*. Glencoe, Ill: Free Press.

———. 1958. *The Protestant Ethic and the Spirit of Capitalism*. Trans. Talcott Parsons. New York: Charles Scribner's Sons.

Williams, Raymond. 1982. *The Sociology of Culture*. New York: Schocken Books.

———. 1983. *Keywords: A Vocabulary of Culture and Society*. Rev. ed. New York: Oxford University Press.

Wilson, Bryan R. 1959. An Analysis of Sect Development. *American Sociological Review* 24.1 (Feb.): 3–15.

———. 1961. *Sects and Society*. Berkeley: University of California Press.

———. 1963a. A Typology of Sects in a Dynamic and Comparative Perspective. *Archives de Sociologie de Religion* 16:49–63. Tran. by Jenny M. Robertson. Reprinted as "A Typology of Sects" in *Sociology of Religion: Selected Readings*. Ed. Roland Robertson. Baltimore: Penguin Books, 1972. Pp. 361–83.

————. 1963b. On the Fringe of Christendom. *Rationalist Annual* 40–50.

————. 1966. *Religion in Secular Society: A Sociological Comment.* London: C. A. Watts.

————. 1978. The Church and Social Change. In *The Church in a Changing Society* 1978:181–86.

————. 1982. *Religion in Sociological Perspective.* Oxford: Oxford University Press.

————. 1990. *The Social Dimensions of Sectarianism: Sects and New Religious Movements in Contemporary Society.* Oxford: Clarendon Press.

Wink, Walter. 1984. *Naming the Powers: The Language of Power in the New Testament.* Philadelphia: Fortress Press.

Yoder, John Howard. 1984. *The Priestly Kingdom: Social Ethics as Gospel.* Notre Dame: University of Notre Dame Press.

————. 1994. *The Royal Priesthood: Essays Ecclesiological and Ecumenical.* Ed. Michael G. Cartwright. Grand Rapids: Eerdmans.

————. 1996. How H. Richard Niebuhr Reasoned: A Critique of *Christ and Culture.* In Stassen, D. M. Yeager, and Yoder 1996:31–89.

Yrigoyen, Charles, Jr., and George H. Bricker, eds. 1978. *Catholic and Reformed: Selected Theological Writings of John Williamson Nevin.* Pittsburgh: Pickwick Press.